End of Myself

The Journey to Resurrection

Danica Reddy

Contents

End of Myself: The Journey to Resurrection

Copyright © 2025 by Danica Reddy

Published under Living Out Your Yes Publishing

ISBN: 979-8-9996708-0-9

All Scripture quotations, unless otherwise noted, are taken from:

To my dear children,

May you never walk the painful roads I once wandered. The blood of the Lamb has redeemed us—and His mercy runs deeper still. May your footsteps be firm, your hearts stay soft, and your lives be marked by surrender. Jesus is worth everything.

Foreword

By Micah Wood

*"You shall be My witnesses when the Holy
Spirit has come upon you." (Acts 1)*

My friend, Danica, is a witness. According to scripture, that
is no small or insignificant task. Witnesses play a profound
role in the advancement of God's kingdom on the earth.
One witness—a woman at a well—unlocked the heart of
entire Samaritan village (John 4:1–42). Another witness—a
preacher in the Judean wilderness—prepared an entire
nation to see Jesus (John 1:29–34). One more witness—a
man raised from the dead—caused the world to go after
Him (see John 12:9–19). Scripture elevates witnesses to the
highest degree of importance and impact.

In fact, all of scripture is a theologically annotated story.
The Bible is the testimony of God's dealings with man. It
recounts His interaction with humanity, detailing what He
has done in history and what He has promised to do in the
future. Those who experience the God of the Bible today
have a duty to add their personal story to the saga—not

because their testimony becomes canonical. But because things happen when people simply talk about what God has done.

David wrote in the Psalms that he would not hide the righteousness, faithfulness, or salvation of God, but talk about it in the congregation (Psalm 40:9–10). Jesus commissioned the demoniac at the Gadarenes, "Tell what great things God has done for you" (Luke 8:38). After His resurrection, rather than immediately revealing Himself to His twelve closest disciples, He entrusted the event to a witness—Mary Magdalene (John 20:17). Likewise, rather than revealing Himself physically to the whole world, He entrusted the message to witnesses (Acts 10:39–43). Danica has engaged in a holy vocation by sharing her story as a personal witness of the living God.

This book is not just a story, but evidence of the Spirit's power on the earth today. That power, though, isn't only effective when working with flawless creatures and sanitized stories. The Spirit's power comes upon and works within earthen vessels. I'm constantly amazed by how honest scripture is about the humanity of the "heroes" of the Bible. It tells more than the highlights of God-feats through patriarchs, prophets, and apostles. It tells their whole story, at least enough of it for us to see their need for repentance. We need scripture's honesty, and in this book, Danica has given us hers.

Danica's honesty immediately had two impacts on my mind. The first is hope. Her story reminds me of a Jason Upton song: "Love Is a Winding Road." Like many of us, Danica's story is not a purely linear process, progressing seamlessly from unchurched heathenism to cleaned up sainthood. It takes twists and turns. It includes break-throughs and setbacks. It's the kind of story that requires and reveals the love of God, which is patient and kind. His love walks down "winding roads" to find us—and He'll even go off road to rescue us from the dark, dark woods. For mankind who is desperately fickle, we need to hear about a God who loves like this.

The second impact of her honesty is awareness. Her story lays bare the schemes of the enemy, whom the Bible names as "that serpent of old" (Rev. 12:9). Through Danica's story you can see the access points he uses, the circumstances he exploits, the lies he likes to tell, and the deception he likes to portray as harmless. For a generation saturated, inundated, and captivated by every opinion imaginable, this awareness of the enemy is key to survival. It shines a light into the shadows where the enemy likes to hide. Danica carries out the charge of Ephesians 5:11, which says to expose the works of darkness.

End of Myself provides one of the things people need most: a reference point. This is a reference point for what it looks like to spiral into the plans of the enemy—even after unde-niable God-encounters. But this is also a reference point for a far greater reality: the beauty of a kind and loving God whose grace doesn't stop when we think it should. Instead, it seems to only be beginning.

Introduction

Before we even get started, I want to remind you of a story from the Gospels.

A man with leprosy came to Jesus. In his world, leprosy meant more than sickness—it meant shame. He was considered unclean. Outcast. Rejected. Unwanted. People saw him as contagious, disgusting, and broken. He lived outside the city, cut off from community and hope. But even in that condition, *he came to Jesus.*

"Now a leper came to Him, imploring Him, kneeling down to Him and saying to Him, 'If You are willing, You can make me clean.' Then Jesus, moved with compassion, stretched out His hand and touched him, and said to him, 'I am willing; be cleansed.'" Mark 1:40–41 (NKJV)

Jesus didn't see what everyone else saw. He didn't recoil. He was moved with compassion. And He didn't just speak healing—He *reached out* and *touched* the man.

He touched the *untouchable.*

He made clean what the world had called unclean.

That's the kind of love you'll find in this story. Not because I'm special, but because *He* is.

I'm not here to offer a polished, poshed up version of my life. I'm here to show you how far grace can reach.

As I reflect on the story God has written in my thirty-something years, I'm overwhelmed—first by His love, then by His unwavering faithfulness. If there's a struggle to be named, I've probably faced it. If there's a breakthrough to be celebrated, I've likely experienced that too. My life has been anything but boring.

I've been stubborn, and I've wrestled with my free will. But oh, the beauty I've found on the other side of surrender, at the end of myself. When I finally said yes to following Jesus, I encountered a love so remarkable and so transformative, that I'll never be the same.

This is a story of cycles—of pain, confusion, searching, and resistance. A journey through inadequacy and desperation that led to a turning point: the moment I came to myself. Just like the prodigal son, I reached the end of me. And there was Jesus—waiting. Not with shame, but with open arms. The cycle broke that day. In Jesus' name, it's finished.

Before you dive in, there's something you should know. This book holds real pieces of my life. Some are raw. Some are still healing. I haven't shared everything—not to hide, but to honor others' privacy and guard the sacred. Some stories are not meant for everyone, and that's okay.

Still, what you *will* find is truth. The kind that set me free. The kind that just might meet you, too. I talk about hard things honestly, but I don't write for shock. I write for healing. Because Jesus didn't just save me—He healed me. And I believe He can do the same for you.

I once walked in deception, believing I was chasing

truth. Like Saul before his conversion to Saint Paul, I thought I was right—but I was so lost. Then Jesus, Light of the World, opened my eyes. And when His light shines, He reveals what's broken—not to shame us, but to heal us. The closer we walk with Him, the more we're called to live differently—set apart, made new, whole.

So, if you're carrying your own weight... if you're aching for clarity, for freedom, for peace...

I pray this book becomes more than just words. I pray it becomes an *invitation* to encounter the living God. Because I didn't *just* survive. I didn't just change. I was rescued. I was touched—even when I shouldn't have been. And I believe He can rescue you too.

So come in close. Take a breath. And let's begin this journey through my life—together.

Chapter 1

The Darkness

I couldn't catch my breath anymore. It was as if every inhale was swallowed before it could reach my lungs. Everywhere I turned there was no answer, no help, no relief. I was beyond tired, beyond weary, beyond hurting. The darkness pressing in on my soul was heavier than anything I had ever known, and I had known plenty of pain.

The weight of who I had become felt like bricks breaking loose in a crumbling foundation. One by one they fell, waiting for the whole structure to collapse. I was alone. Desperately, unavoidably, absolutely alone. What had I done?

"Danica, seriously. How have you become such an idiot? Do you even see what you are doing with your life? There is no hope for you anymore. You are done."

The voice was not audible, but it might as well have been screamed in my face. The accusations beat against my mind in relentless waves. My children were better off with their grandparents, I thought. They were safer there. I was so inadequate that they did not even live with me anymore. My husband was probably relieved any moment he did not have to see my face. My dad was gone. My mom was hundreds of miles away. My friends had their own lives, and months had passed since I had truly talked to anyone. Who would even notice if I was gone?

Work? I was performing well, finally hitting numbers that looked impressive on paper, but sleeping alone in hotel rooms night after night made even my best wins feel hollow. It would not matter if I disappeared; they could replace me in a day. My life meant nothing.

And yet, though I could not feel it, God's grace was already present. His love hovered close, waiting for me to let Him in. Even in this suffocating darkness, He had not left. But I did not believe I was worth rescuing.

My desire to be free and live "my life" had ended in chains. All the chasing after what the world promised—self-fulfillment, adventure, pleasure—had left me trapped in despair. Living "my truth" had been nothing more than a slow death.

Anxiety gnawed at my insides. Depression pulled me deeper into its pit. On the outside, I could fake it. Inside, I was drowning. I wanted the darkness to swallow me whole.

I told myself I couldn't do it anymore. I couldn't keep living like this. Every step felt like walking through quicksand. Another night at the bar, another drink until I could not take another sip, none of it brought peace. The people at the bar did not care about me. They would not remember me tomorrow. This was not who I was raised to be.

And the things I was doing? They were not even what I truly wanted. Nothing could help me now. I was a waste. I had ruined my life, and worse, I had ruined my children's lives by being the kind of mother they did not deserve. My husband needed someone whole, someone better.

I stayed in bed for days, buried under a blanket that felt

as heavy as the air in my lungs. No photo could stir up hope. No thought of the future could survive here. I wanted to escape—not for a night, but forever. I was misunderstood, misguided, and disheartened. Even if I told someone how I was feeling, they wouldn't understand. Everything I had done in life had failed. Honestly, I couldn't name one thing I had completed well. Basically, everything in my life that I had signed up for was left incomplete or marked as a failure.

The lies came like daggers. They pierced through my mind and into my spirit, each one sinking deeper than the last. And I believed them. I trusted them more than the truths I had once staked my life on. I gave in and let the daggers pierce through every bit of sense I had left. Then I made up my mind—I just needed to move on and let the world be free of me. I was a complete and utter failure and deserved nothing more. A waste of breath. A waste of time. At the bottom of a spiral, and there was no way up. The only way out was to leave; it was the best decision for my family, for everyone. The world would be better without me. My family would be free of my failures. My children would never have to watch me keep falling. It was the only way forward.

So, I did what I needed to do. *I left.*

Chapter 2

The Threshold

Eventually, the thoughts were silenced. Finally, it was happening. The weight was lifted as my soul began to leave my body. I could hear the chaos and panic going on, but I no longer cared.

I was floating. Up, up... further away.

What was that peace? It was better than sleeping. It was warmth, it was light, but also dark. It kept going deeper, yet the floating felt higher. I could hear myself breathing—short, labored breaths accompanied by a rattle in the back of my throat, a sound I had once recognized from watching my dad die.

Sheer panic rushed over me as I realized it was done. The darkness that coincided with light overcame me. Could this be it? I fought between those moments and all of eternity, all while my body lay frozen, no longer able to respond to the nurses taking care of me.

There was so much left unsaid. Undone.

My kids—oh my God, my kids. What had I done? I regretted it instantly. How had I been so stupid? I thought I knew what I wanted. This wasn't it. My soul began to shift beyond this world.

There was no going back. I kept floating. Things grew black, then light.

God, have mercy.

I could barely think it. It was over. That was the end. I was gone, and I could hardly reason or understand anything anymore. It was just... nothing. I wondered if I would go see Jesus first, or if I'd end up straight in hell. My soul was crushed. I was so embarrassed. I hadn't wanted to be bad—this wasn't what I wanted. I didn't want to be separated from God. I was just so tired. I was hurting.

And now I was moving somewhere. My soul was gone. I recognized I was no longer on the cold table in that Texas emergency department, but suspended in an abyss. I could still faintly hear the sounds below. I recognized the panic of the nurses as they questioned me, and had noticed their disgruntled faces before it all went black.

Everything in my life that had led to this point was over. It couldn't be. It was over.

As I hovered in that moment between life and death, I knew that God's mercy was the only thing keeping me tethered to this world. I wasn't meant to leave just yet; He had a purpose for me, even in that darkness. Slowly, I felt the immense grip of fear release.

> "So do not fear, for I am with you; do not be dismayed, for I am your God. I will strengthen you and help you; I will uphold you with my righteous right hand." —Isaiah 41:10 (NIV)

"We've got sinus rhythm!"

I felt myself back on the table, unable to respond, but present with my lingering thoughts.

"What the.... just happened? Did I just die?"

Chapter 3

The Shattering

I f you saw me and my friends in the summertime as kids, it was almost guaranteed we'd be in the swimming pool in my backyard, baptizing each other and preaching to the horses. We'd jump out of the pool and dance around "in the Holy Ghost" on the deck, then cannonball back in like the little Pentecostals we were. That was childhood, and it was so much fun.

I didn't know it then, but those moments, saturated in Spirit and sunshine, would become the anchor I'd return to when everything else fell apart.

I grew up in rural, very rural Alabama. I was the daughter of a country man who had been radically saved and delivered from a heavy lifestyle of drug addiction and shenanigans, and a "city slicker" mama who wasn't really from the city at all, but from the next town over. That was where we went if we needed the bank or the church. At least that town had a red light, so my dad called it a city and teased my mom for not growing up picking cotton like he did. She was also eighteen years younger than him, so life was never boring.

My mom got saved first at a little Thursday night prayer meeting in Jasper, Alabama, at a Christian bookstore called The Shepherd's Place. I was already born, and I'm pretty sure she dragged me with her sometimes. I remember getting in trouble for stealing and eating pencil erasers. Yes, I was a handful. I was too young to understand the details of the time between her salvation and my dad's, but I know she eventually left him for a while because he wouldn't follow Jesus. We stayed somewhere else for a time.

Something must have changed, though, because I don't remember growing up any other way than in the church. My daddy was the kind of Christian who would love and employ all kinds of "heathens," but he also held them accountable and told them about Jesus. He had been so impacted by the Lord that I can't separate my earliest memories from church life. I can still smell the sawdust and feel the woodchips from the floors of old tent revivals. I can hear the organ blaring old hymns and remember New Year's Eve watch night services and week-long "conventions" during camp meetings.

I saw people give their lives to Jesus every Sunday. I was used to walking out of children's church during altar calls because there was never a Sunday where God wasn't moving. Our church was a safe place of repentance, fire, Holy Ghost power, and revival.

Until one day, it wasn't.

The first time I felt my world shatter wasn't at home, or even in the hands of those who hurt me behind closed doors. It was in the church. I had been abused by people I knew, in ways no little girl should ever experience. There were wounds buried so deep I've probably forgotten some of them. But somehow, none of that mattered when I was at church. When we sang, *When I think of His goodness and what He's done for me*, I didn't just sing—I danced, shouted, and spun until my head hurt. We had Holy Ghost-led meetings where heaven touched earth, and in those sacred moments, the pain was hidden away. In church, I was safe. I had a family. I had Jesus.

And for a while... that was enough.

Until it wasn't.

I remember the night the church held a meeting to "cast out" the pastor—my pastor, the man I loved like my own grandfather. I was just a kid, but I knew something was wrong. The church split down the middle, and so did my heart. My family told me one version of the story. Other families told theirs. None of it made sense to me.

How could people who danced in the Spirit one Sunday be screaming at each other the next? How could the holy hands of a deacon throw drills at a youth pastor's head? It was the first time I realized that God's people didn't always act like God. And that realization broke something in me.

I loved that place. I lived for every kids' crusade and altar call. I ran up and down the halls like they belonged to me. I preached pretend sermons in the Sunday school room while my mom was in choir practice, using the green chalkboard to illustrate my little heart out. I led puppet shows for the younger kids, begged to be on the drama team, and did anything I could to serve the Lord—because I believed I was His.

I can still hear Sister Darlene's prayer when she'd hold up a sponge and have us say, "God, make us like a sponge and let us soak up Your Word... but squeeze out everything that's not of You." I prayed that with all my heart. I believed it. I was a sponge, through and through.

That church wasn't just a building. It was my foundation.

And when it cracked, so did I.

The church may have broken my heart, but Jesus held me together. He never promised people would be perfect, but He promised He would never leave me. Even when the people who were supposed to show me Christ's love failed, He remained faithful, and His love became my refuge.

But when my dad said we would never go back, that the friends and family I loved were no longer good, and that I couldn't talk to them anymore, I was confused. And I was beyond crushed. There was no pain like it. I never thought we would recover.

What I didn't know then was that these cracks in my foundation, this collision of faith and failure, would one day become the story God used most. But in that moment, all I knew was loss.

Chapter 4

The Search

After that, we started "church hopping" to find the best church to go to. The one that had the best choir, the best preaching, the best youth group, who handled money well, who catered to the Holy Spirit, and did everything perfectly. We looked around a lot.

We finally found another church that was founded after the church split, which we had been a part of. After church hopping and "visiting around," we went there and got rooted in that church, until they told us we couldn't pray in tongues anymore, and then that church split too. It crushed my dad, because the pastor there was someone that he had led to the Lord personally, and he was so proud of him. And then he wasn't.

Looking back, God has used it to make me understand that He was always meant to be my true anchor. While people and institution could let me down, He was always there. Through it all, He was teaching me to build my life on Him alone, not on things that could crumble.

After the second major church split, we visited for a little while and went to a denominational church. God forbid, we had always been non-denominational and for a good reason, I thought. By this time, I was about 15, and I tried my best to fit in with the new youth group. But I was a heavy teenager at this time, very overweight, and a little bit of an outcast. Getting involved with yet another youth group seemed like a waste of time. No group could ever replace the group I grew up with, and no one else would accept me.

But after a while, I got to know a few people and started fitting in, kind of. But sadly, this is where I really got introduced to alcohol.

At 15 years old, I went to my first party, even though all the years before that I had been shielded from it due to my parents' past deliverance from drugs and alcohol. But because the kid throwing the party was in my youth group, my parents let me go, not knowing what would happen. I'm sure they also were hoping I would finally fit in. That was the first night I got drunk on alcohol, and of all things, Jäger-meister. I'll never forget it.

I can't lie to you, though the taste was not that great, the feeling of that first time was such a nice feeling. I was full of courage. I felt cool, and it didn't matter that I was the freshman in the room with all seniors. Alcohol helped me fit in and made me feel good, until it didn't. This continued for a little while, and I'd tell my parents I was going to a prayer meeting over the weekend, and my youth group friends, and I would party and be wicked little ones, but don't worry, we would worship and pray on Sunday. I really did feel bad sometimes, though, and my heart was very conflicted. I knew I was wrong, but in the south, church can be more important than Jesus sometimes, so I was still doing the right thing. Plus, if I really thought about it, the Bible didn't say *exclusively* that I couldn't drink, but then again, I was only fifteen.

But after a while, my dad noticed a change in me and he saw that it was not right. He ended up pulling me from that church, too. Desperate for a church family and something to do on Sundays, he brought me somewhere else. What I didn't know was that my old friends from my childhood church went there and had been telling the pastors to pray for me. So, sure enough, when I got there, the pastor had no shame in calling me to the front of the church and inviting me to rededicate my life to Jesus. I was so embarrassed. Even though I was 16 or 17 at this point, I didn't really think I had "fallen away" from God. I was just kind of having fun, I thought. But mental battles plagued my mind, and my root system was no longer that deep. So, when the pastor asked me to rededicate my life to God in front of everyone I knew, I did. But the next day, I went back to school and drank alcohol in my "lemonade" bottle during 4th period to get through the day. I was weak, but in my heart, I wanted to do what was right.

Somewhere in that time, my family was going through a severe spiritual attack. I was struggling with the will to live, and one day while I was hungover, headed to color guard practice, I wrecked my car into a brick mailbox, and when I went to tell my dad, he just broke down and said, "the devil's been trying to get me to kill myself" and I was so shocked that my daddy had struggles. It was then I considered that maybe since my daddy didn't want to live, maybe that's why I didn't want to live sometimes either. I didn't know until later how things can be affected generationally.

Fast forward a little, life was a constant rollercoaster for me. It was like fire and water, all the time. I'd been baptized with the Holy Spirit, experienced some incredible emotional healing, and had amazing encounters with the Lord. I even led so many people to Christ in high school. But then, I'd cuss a little here and there and struggle with alcohol and suicidal thoughts. One moment, I'd be ON FIRE, and the next, I'd just want to give up and die. No matter what I did, I couldn't get it right, and I couldn't be consistent.

Chapter 5

The Fire

When the time finally came to graduate high school, I had a teacher tell me that I'd never make it out of the town, or even the county I grew up in, and that basically I'd be a lowlife. This same teacher had spent the last four years calling out my inconsistencies and calling me a hypocrite and he challenged my beliefs about God. He also persuaded me to think deeper than just what I'd learned in church throughout my High School years. I'm actually thankful for him, and value his teachings and challenges more than he'll ever know. He's one of the few people who was honest with me even though it was custom to just smile and say, "Praise God, sister" and go on about your day.

I was determined to make something of myself, and fueled by frustration, I made an internal vow that I wouldn't stay in Alabama all my life. I'd go wherever I could, if God would use me. I knew I could be better than that. I knew that I had a calling on my life.

Giving up my dream to be the first one in my family with a college degree, I ripped up my college acceptance letters and went off to ministry school... in another part of Alabama. I'll never forget receiving my acceptance letter to ministry school. It was the same day that North Alabama had devastating tornadoes. Forced to be home in the dark with my parents, I was so anxious waiting on a decision from a school they didn't know I had even applied to. I walked to the mailbox to escape the musty house that had no electricity. I wept walking back up the driveway reading the letter as my destiny spelled out before me.

The school was close enough to home that I was able to drive back and forth 45 minutes each way every day. I'd use that time to pray or practice memorizing the scriptures the instructors assigned. It was a beautiful time. The teaching was mind blowing to me. Different from anything I'd heard in all my years, in all the different churches. Pressure was put on us to grow spiritually and in our character. As I developed into a stronger, more mature believer, I was staying out of my sin cycles and feeling good.

But then in the early part of my first year, that ministry also went through their own "church split" of sorts and though it didn't affect me directly, the situation triggered many memories of my church splits from earlier on in my life and I was a "triggered" wreck for a while. I'll never forget hyperventilating over my small group leader's sofa because a leader was leaving (one I had never even spoken to).

In that season, though I grew, many of my darkest flaws surfaced. Many times, when God wants to heal us, He will expose our issues. While triggered, I became clingy to people in my life, desperate to make sure I somehow felt loved, and I sought their approval in hopes they wouldn't leave my life, too. I was gripped by insecurity and fear. The Lord exposed that behavior in me to heal it. But all I had known for the previous 5 or 6 years of life prior to ministry school was that what had once been stable and secure in my life (the church) was now inconsistent and unreliable.

Thankfully, this ministry I was a part of didn't have a "normal" church at that time. I did, however, spend all my days in classes, volunteering, and working when I could. Coming late in the evenings and burning myself out from living 45 minutes away from campus when I could've just found a place to live there... I was a tired student, but I was very thankful. I did grow and overcome a lot in that year, which became foundational to me. I also grew in experience as I served in various aspects of the ministries. Other students weren't always able to get to see the parts of the different ministries I saw, and I was so thankful. I was able to see what it was like to both serve and sustain a worldwide ministry through product management and creation, bookstore sales, events, praying for people, cleaning the facilities, making CD series (I know, we don't use CDs anymore, but they used to be cool) and so much more. It was such a joy to serve and gave me so much fulfillment.

I had some of the best days of my life and sat under some of the most incredible leadership you could ever sit under. Even people whom I had grown up watching on TV would lead prayer meetings, worship, preach at church services (they eventually started a church), or even teach our classes. I'll be honest, I was starstruck sometimes (most times). But the best classes were the ones when the Holy Spirit would take over. I was marked again and again by encounter. I was so deeply honored to be in the room, and I learned a lot.

Chapter 6

The Encounters

"Where shall I go from your Spirit? Or where shall I flee from your presence? If I ascend to heaven, you are there! If I make my bed in Sheol, you are there! If I take the wings of the morning and dwell in the uttermost parts of the sea, even there your hand shall lead me, and your right hand shall hold me." (Psalm 139:7–10 ESV)

I didn't always feel Him, and I certainly didn't always seek Him, but He was there. Always. In the good, in the bad, in the ugly and unmentionable, His presence lingered like a breath I didn't realize I was holding. Even when I ran, He followed. Even when I fell, He held on. He was so present that in my darkest places, I was sometimes angry I couldn't hide from Him. And though I didn't deserve Him, He never once let me go.

Some encounters with the Lord have marked me so deeply, they've stayed with me for decades.

Ministry school was incredible and life-changing, but it was not where my encounters with God began. Even before that, the Lord touched me in ways I can only describe as supernatural. I always had a "knowing" that God would use me, and I cried out for Him to do so. I often had dreams—some warning me, others speaking life to me.

For a while, I had a recurring dream about a huge python that slept in my room. It would hide under my pillow, and though I knew it was there, it didn't bother me. I'd ask others to help capture or kill it, but everyone else in the dream seemed helpless. Then one night, the dream shifted. The snake began squeezing me so tightly I could hardly breathe. I jolted awake—and to my shock, my old Gateway desktop computer had somehow dialed up the internet on its own in the middle of the night. My YouTube page was open to a Jentezen Franklin sermon titled "The Spirit of Python." It was supernatural, and I was wrecked. That night, God delivered me from alcohol.

Another time, I became suddenly aware that I had unforgiveness toward people in my childhood who had abused me. The realization hit me hard—so hard it turned into hatred. I shared this with my pastor's wife, and she prayed with me. For six days I wrestled with God, trying to forgive. On the seventh day, at youth camp, I encountered the Holy Spirit in a way few people ever do. I was so deeply touched by God that I was delivered from hatred in an instant—and then I couldn't speak English for over 24 hours. I didn't sleep. I prayed, shook, cried, and spoke in tongues all night.

Eventually, my prayer language began to shift. I heard myself speaking in other languages, and by the Spirit, I understood my own prayers for nations I had never seen. I was just a country girl from Alabama who had never met a missionary—yet that night, God told me I would be one.

Then something happened that I didn't fully understand until years later.

In that moment at youth camp, my heart broke beyond what I thought possible for other nations. I began to groan in the Spirit, feeling their pain and weeping on their behalf. I saw the faces of people I had never met before—faces etched in my soul. I didn't know how I would ever reach them, but I knew I had to go.

Years later, standing on foreign soil with a camera in my hand, I snapped a simple photo of a crowd. When I looked at it later, I froze. The faces in that picture were the very same faces I had seen as a teenager in that encounter with God—the same expressions, the same intensity in their eyes. It was as if God had reached back through time and pulled the thread of His story taut, showing me that what He spoke years earlier had been real all along. That moment undid me. It reminded me that no encounter with God ever stands alone; each one is part of a story He has been writing from the very beginning.

One of my favorite encounters from those years still makes me laugh. I was at the fifth or sixth church we had attended, during a planned weeklong revival. The same evangelist came every year, and he was always full of energy. On this occasion, he preached the entire message wearing a prison outfit. I don't remember much about the sermon, but I remember I had been leading a Bible study at school with two girls who had been praying to be baptized in the Holy Spirit with the evidence of speaking in tongues. Both had received the gift before me, and I was growing impatient.

Before that service, I prayed in my very country Alabama accent, "Now God, You said You gave us the Holy Spirit, and in the Bible You didn't withhold Him from anybody, and I want the baptism of the Holy Spirit, and I want to speak in tongues!" I imagine my persistent prayers (and that accent) even pushed my friends to pray for me to receive the gift.

That night, the evangelist gave a very specific altar call —probably unrelated to me—but I went forward anyway. He walked up, took off his prison outfit, wrapped it in his hand, and smacked me with it. The next thing I knew, I was flying backwards, speaking in tongues. Only God.

Those were just a few of the encounters I had with Him in my teen years. After I graduated high school, my walk with the Lord deepened even more. I experienced freedom from fear, intimidation, and feelings of abandonment. I began to walk more closely with Him, learning the discipline of a believer. I heard His voice—beautiful, steady, leading me in the right direction.

But sometimes... I also disobeyed that voice.

Chapter 7

The Drift

"Sin will take you farther than you want to go, keep you longer than you want to stay, and cost you more than you want to pay." — *Unknown*

Ministry school was supposed to fix me. I thought I was good. I'd be fine, at least I thought. But I wasn't. After my first year of ministry school, I went full-time at my then-existing job in the medical field, and though I knew I should've done a second year, I decided that I was the one who knew best. I didn't really ask the Lord; I just assumed that if I went where I wanted to go, He'd follow. I had already had a good walk with God, learned some more of the Bible, was filled with the Holy Spirit, had some good stories, and in my mind, I was ready. I didn't need any additional ministry training; I would do fine. I went on to nursing school and struck out at that, but I did find a church that wasn't really the best place for me. I dabbled in ministry here and there, leading worship, speaking off and on, and doing whatever I could to serve God. I jumped on some Christian trends and that's really when the deconstruction movement started so prevalently.

I had some cool experiences, saw some miracles, really stepped out into evangelism, made some friends, and even lost some weight. That season was beautiful, but somehow it grew dark. I began to question foundational values, the validity of scriptures, and felt it healthy to have a God I could question. Something happened, and sadly, some of the friends I spent my time with studying the Bible with at one point became the same friends I started partying with again. They happened to also be from that original youth group that introduced me to alcohol. I slowly drifted back into old habits and relapsed back into a lifestyle of sin, but this time I went just a little deeper. Depression had always had a grip on me, but I was silent about it. I was a Christian, and now I had been in ministry, so I couldn't tell anyone. That realization isolated me, and with being outside of the will of God for my life, I felt that, and it weighed heavily on me.

On the outside, I had grown to look successful. No one in my life would have guessed I was struggling. But I was suffocating on the inside. I even felt this lingering in my physical body. For the first time in my life, I found myself struggling with mental disorders and got on antidepressants. I also struggled physically and had an ailment that doctors finally concluded to be a "Fever of Unknown Origin". For three months, with no medical reasoning, my body was weak, febrile, and I also suffered from heavy migraines and body pains. I didn't have the flu, I didn't have a tumor, and thousands of dollars' worth of diagnostic testing revealed that I didn't have any diagnosis. I thought I was dying, so my doctor prescribed me an antidepressant, which also did not help. I stopped taking it. The symptoms did go away eventually, though, and it's still a medical mystery.

Unfortunately, though, all the recurrent migraines assisted me in a secret opioid dependence, but it was a 'minor' dependance, so I thought I was still okay. At first, other medications helped, and then they didn't. Then the pain pills helped, then they didn't. But they did make me feel a little better. So, I kept taking them. As time progressed, I ended up stepping down from ministry, knowing something was wrong and I was in no position to lead. The isolation after that grew.

As time went on, and darkness consumed my soul, I danced with death time and time again. After overdosing one day, I laid on the floor, paralyzed, covered in my own urine, watching the ceiling fan move in a way that seemed like time had basically stopped. I knew I couldn't do life like that anymore. I couldn't move or speak, so I just thought, "God, this can't be the end." I guess I fell asleep and woke up normally, because I don't really remember a lot about that time. I am certain the Lord has helped me not to be affected by those memories, because truly, I don't remember.

I wasn't too suicidal during that time in my life. It wasn't really a desire to leave this world, but instead to numb the emotions that resulted from it. However, one day I did have enough, and I wanted to go away forever, not just to sleep. I had thought about it before, and had had tormenting thoughts, but had not tried to go through with it. But on one Memorial Day night, with what felt like an aimless, empty life, I had a fail-proof plan as I made my permanent escape plan. As I thought about it, the darkness and pain I carried in my soul were too much to carry. The idea of escape allured me in as the burden was too grand. I was no longer walking in the will of God, and that bothered me. I failed at ministry and that bothered me. Many people had hurt me, and that bothered me. There were people I loved and lost that absolutely broke me. The heartbreaks. The devastation. The feeling of failing, time and time again. The idea that I was living completely outside the plan of God for my life. It all haunted me.

I was living in my own house, which my dad had given me. I had always wanted to grow up, get married, and have twelve children, but the person I had wanted to spend the rest of my life with didn't really love me back and had shattered my already fragile heart. I was empty and devastated. I had lost sight of a once favorite scripture.

"Trust in the Lord with all your heart and lean not on your own understanding; in all your ways submit to him, and he will make your paths straight." —Proverbs 3:5-6 (NIV)

My trust was no longer in God. Since I felt like I wouldn't get married or have much else in life, I asked my dad for an early inheritance, and he obliged. I was tired that Memorial Day and had a bottle of cheap vodka next to me, a bottle of pills, and an old pistol my dad had given me to protect myself since I now lived alone. The crushed-up pills in lines across the coffee table and shot glasses lined up with the gun at the end. I just knew I was finished. I would take a shot and do a line. Then I'd text a friend. "Hey, hope you're well. I just wanted you to know I love you. And I'm thankful for you." Repeat. Halfway into my robot-like execution, the buzz was feeling good, and I don't know what happened, but I guess I forgot what I was doing. When I texted one of my closest friends, instead of sticking to the standard script, I simply said, "Hey, what are you up to?" And somehow that turned into her telling me to come over.

Thank God for Holy Ghost-filled friends. And how thankful I am for the Holy Ghost! While I was both drunk and high, I don't know how I made the 45-minute drive to her house, or even the walk up the steps to her second-floor apartment. But I do know that as I walked into her home, the tangible presence of the Lord was so strong that in an instant, I became completely sober. I'm not kidding. I was not fine, and then suddenly I was. I felt the presence of God stronger than I had in a long time, and the girl had just opened the door and let me sit on her couch! I began to confess everything to her, and later that night, I reached out to some leaders in my life, and they within days helped me get detoxed and into a faith-based rehab.

A few days later, just a short time after my 21st birthday, I found myself completely detoxed and driving down to Pensacola, FL, to go to rehab. What in the world? Who was I? How embarrassing.

Chapter 8

The Slamma

I can't really tell you my story without including some stuff from my time in rehab, which I lovingly nicknamed "The Slamma," even though it wasn't really jail.

But before we go into that, let me just say, the enemy has literally tried to kill me all my life. And the Lord has always been merciful. I can't tell you how many wrecks we had when I was a kid. There was multiple. One time, I was just a toddler and it's a wonder my mother and I both didn't die. In the 90s, the child restraints and laws surrounding them that we have today were nonexistent. Because my mom needed to feed me, she put me in the front seat instead of the backseat that day, and she was feeding me McDonald's French fries when she wrecked the car, it spun around and flipped multiple times in the air and crushed the back seat where I should have and always sat.

We walked away with no scratch. The car, however, was in a tree and destroyed.

Another time, my dad and I were driving back in our old Buick from a cow sale, and a car slammed us into another car, causing a 5-car pile-up. When we crashed, I was reading Psalms to my dad out loud from my little Gideon Bible I had gotten from Vacation Bible School. The firefighters told us that the Lord stopped the car at the exact speed we needed it to stop to preserve our lives.

There were also the many wrecks I got into as a teenager from driving too fast. Hitting dogs from out of nowhere, deer jumping in the road, mailboxes, fences, etc., you name it. I don't know why my parents kept letting me drive. They should've pulled the keys, but hey, I'm good now.

Regarding death, there's also the time that I almost got kidnapped at the thrift store, and a man threatened me with a gun to get out of the car and come with him. Or the time someone shot me with a pellet gun, pierced my brand-new shoes, and then went and got a big boy gun to aim at my head, but I somehow got away. And then there's the big one, where I *actually died.*

But back to rehab, a place I believe God used to keep me from such similar situations in that time in my life. A sanctuary, though never in my whole life have I hated a place more than that. Looking back, I'm also very thankful for it and it was helpful. But gosh it was hard. It's that year of my life, when I had to put down the good girl facade and realize that I was truly and utterly hopeless without the Lord. You see, until this point, even in my sin, I was the "good" girl. No one knew anything of my galavants, and I was an absolute master at behavior modification. I was Danny and Mandy's girl, and I was a *"pretty good young lady."*

At this point, now that I had been to ministry school, I thought I was even better than the rest of the people in town. Though I was not in ministry and was just living a normal life, I was still good. I was working a good job, being nice to people, and did whatever my parents asked of me for the most part. No one knew of my sins. I wasn't necessarily trying to lie about it, either. But I did compartmentalize my pain and did whatever I needed to numb it. I stayed the good girl, even though I did bad things.

In fact, when I told my parents I was going to rehab, they were so shocked that they told me I was being brainwashed to believe something was wrong with me, so I could get far away from them. I really was pained by their reaction and that even made me feel more betrayed. I was shocked, but from the days spent shaking, sweating, and vomiting from detoxing prior to that, I had some indication that I wasn't brainwashed. As I was leaving, my dad told me that if I walked out the door of his house, I could never come back. That was a bad day, and I did walk out, but thank God he did end up letting me come back.

God had his plans, His grace started creating a path for me even though I was unaware of it at that time. Through His mercy I found a place where I could finally begin my journey toward restoration.

The 6-hour road trip south was fun, but daunting. I was okay mostly, but I couldn't articulate how deeply sad I was knowing that my friends joining me on that trip would continue their lives without me once they dropped me off. The same people who took me to rehab were also the people who helped me detox for a week. They were the people who helped me see that there was more to my problems than just a little alcohol dependence. And though listening to them and uprooting my life and throwing aside the "good girl" title by admitting I needed help was a great risk, getting help was the right decision and I was ready, but I desperately needed people with me. I couldn't be all alone again. So, I laughed as much as I could on the trip down, but after what felt faster than it was, we made it into Pensacola.

In my typical delusion, I was excited to come to a new city, and my friends helped me make the best of my goodbye by allowing me to join them on one adventure. We all went to the beach and had a nice lunch. Then we made the trip I had dreaded the most, and we drove over to the Women's Center that I'd call my new home for the next twelve months. There would be no hangouts with friends, no phone, no money, no job, no independence, no freedom. It was just me, God, demons, and a bunch of drug addicts in a cold, concrete dorm with bunk beds. What had I done?

Still, I walked through those doors with a no turning back attitude. I was surrounded by a whole group of people supporting me (I mean, honestly, who else walks up into a program with six people supporting them), but I sobbed like a baby when they left. It was a mix of relief and fear. I knew being there was good, but I was sad my identity was now crushed. Everything came crashing in when I sat on the couch without them and realized where I was. It was over-whelming to say goodbye to my friends, to say the least. I was more vulnerable at that moment than I'd ever been in my life, and I'd dare to say it continues to be one of the scariest days of my life to date.

I was not anticipating how much structure there would be in the program. I was used to rules growing up, but boy, did they have lots of extra rules that didn't always make sense. I came into the program with another girl on the same day, but people who joined the program within the same few weeks of each other weren't really allowed to be alone or talk to each other much. I understand that though, because until then, I didn't really know the recipe for making meth. But I learned it. I mean, that specific girl didn't teach me, but talk happens.

The staff and my counselors were aware of the pastors who brought me into the program and knew my history and reputation. I was expecting that to give me a little favor, but it did not. In fact, they also did not give one care that I could quote Psalm 91 or Ephesians 1 & 2. They didn't care that I made 100% on all my Bible class papers or excelled "academically" in the program. They didn't care that when I spoke, wisdom came out, or that my addictions were somehow "less" than others, or that my struggles didn't seem as blatant.

When I went to the counseling sessions, I was an open book. Blaming my addictions on past traumas and abuse, painting them the pictures of memories that didn't hurt so much to pull up, but seemed deep. But the leaders in the program challenged me deeply day by day and called out my bologna time and time again. They didn't care who I had been. They were calling me to walk in the higher calling on my life and not some made up version that protected me.

I don't think anyone else in the program got in as much trouble as I did for behavior modification and "being good". That was so annoying. So, then I tried to be bad. After a few months in the program, things weren't really progressing, and a breakthrough wasn't happening, so I decided to let it rip and be a little rebellious here and there. Simple things, really. Just not listening and allowing myself to dabble in other struggles that I hadn't openly struggled with before, but other people in the house maybe did. It was a continuous battleground, and I was defiant.

I was always in trouble. For being good, being bad. Being indifferent. For harming myself. I had to write multiple essays, do extra service work, lost the little privileges I had, and there were weeks when I would wear a neon yellow shirt with a scripture on the back of it, which meant people weren't allowed to speak with me. You could answer questions in class, and go to your counseling sessions, but essentially, it felt like it was a stone-walling t-shirt at best. But the idea was meant to help you go inward and speak with the Lord instead of your peers. It was probably equally harmful and beneficial depending on the day.

I also tried to escape the program and left many times. The furthest I ever got was to the fence line, though, because where would I go? I had friends who had threatened to leave the program, but because they were court-ordered to be there, I ended up being the "student driver" who had to drop them off at a homeless shelter with all their belongings in a black garbage bag.

Heartbreaking, honestly.

I also have never seen so many demons in my life. Believe what you will, but we saw them. We heard them. And sometimes, we would have so much warfare in the house that a few of us would be physically ill or with scratches on us. We always knew when a new girl came in, even if we hadn't seen her yet. Because a lot of times, even if she had detoxed, her first few nights in the program, demons would manifest during our nightly 7 pm worship time. Screams and shrieks would fill the house, and tongues would erupt from the ones who had already fought their demons and been delivered. You'll never experience anything like a holy ghost-filled drug rehabilitation center, unless you experience it. It's not for the weak or faint of heart, I'll tell you that.

That time in my life was crucial, though. Though my addictions weren't as "strong" or as "life controlling" as those of others who were my sisters, the depravity of who I was without Jesus was just the same. I was probably a way harder case than most of the girls in the program because it took me a good six or seven months to even accept that I had an issue and repent.

I can laugh at it now, but they nicknamed me "the hot mess." Because I certainly was, and I struggled with some serious issues while in the program. Even thinking back, I am so thankful for God's mercy that kept me when I didn't deserve it. I am thankful that I was in a safe place while I dealt with things like cutting and self-harm, deep anxiety attacks, same sex attraction, rebellion, depression, and deep-rooted rejection. Some of the other things I endured in my time in the program were more than I want to put down in black and white, but I did get my feelings hurt a lot, and I had a lot of traumas that I had to deal with. I also watched the same be true for others as they got hurt.

Almost daily, someone would have an emotional break-down, as it wasn't a house full of perfect angels. We were a group of broken and contrite ladies, with stories that would absolutely break your heart. But God used that season in my life to save me and my sisters, repeatedly. He also used that time to help my own blood family open up about our troubles, because in my whole life, we didn't talk about issues—we just pretended they didn't exist.

Chapter 9

The Missed Call

One thing I hadn't anticipated struggling with so intensely in rehab was the weight of squandered dreams. The ache of knowing I had once tasted the life I was called to live, only to lose it, felt heavier than I could carry.

Exactly one year before entering the program, I had gone on my first mission trip to Honduras. Even though I was no longer at ministry school, they still let me join the team. It was my first time stepping into a different culture—bright colors lining the streets, voices speaking a language I didn't understand, children with eyes full of hope for a future they couldn't yet see.

Each day we went into schools, classrooms packed with eager, curious faces. We shared the good news of Jesus, prayed with the children, and invited them to the crusade at the end of the week. I can still remember kneeling beside tiny desks, holding small hands, and seeing their faces light up when they prayed to know the Lord.

On the final night, the open field was filled with thousands who had come to hear the gospel. When the invitation was given, people streamed forward. Families wept together. Men fell to their knees. Children lifted their hands high. I stood there, taking it all in, knowing God was moving in ways I could never fully put into words. That night marked me. It was the kind of moment you carry for the rest of your life.

But now, one year later, my greatest achievement was working in the back of a dusty thrift store with no AC, sorting through boxes of musty donations in my yellow vest. Afternoons meant standing on concrete floors for hours, breathing in dust, surrounded by chipped mugs, mismatched shoes, and clothes that smelled like mildew. The thought of more crusades, more open fields, more souls coming to Jesus felt impossibly far away.

Honduras had been full of light, joy, and purpose. Here, I was just another resident in a recovery program, living in depression, pain, and bondage instead of walking in the gospel. I knew the call of God on my life, yet here I was, miles away from it in every sense.

I carried that grief almost until the end of my program, believing I had ruined my chance, that the testimony God had given me was now tainted. But as graduation drew closer, something began to shift. I started to make real progress. Healing was happening. Hope was taking root again.

And the more I thought about what might come next, the more I realized this wasn't only about whether my calling could be restored. It was about my heart. Could I trust God again? And could He trust me? Honduras had lit something in me that no amount of failure could fully snuff out. The ache for that life was growing too loud to ignore.

Chapter 10

The Breakthrough

By the time I sat across from my counselor for one of our sessions, I was carrying more questions than answers. My days were packed with rules, routines, and hard work, but deep inside, fear and shame still knotted me up. God had already used people to guide me before, but this felt different. I could sense He was about to dig right down to the root.

There are moments in life when a single conversation changes everything. For me, one of those moments happened in that office. Her words didn't just speak to me —they sliced right through the confusion, fear, and excuses I had been hiding behind, and called me into freedom.

God gives us the gift of people like this, people who walk in at the exact right time and leave a mark you never forget. That season became one of the most pivotal of my life.

"Okay, okay! I am so angry at God! How dare He let me go through all of that?!" My voice was almost a shout. "How could He just let me lose my childhood and then expect me to serve Him? I didn't ask for any of this. I didn't even ask to be a Christian."

Tears pressed to the surface as I spoke this honestly to Mrs. A for the first time. I had been raised to believe I needed God. But what if I didn't? What if I didn't have to have Him? What if this whole thing was a lie?

"I trust Him... I think. But I don't want to. I don't even want to like Him. In fact, I am angry at God. There. That's the truth."

I stared into the corner of her office, almost daring Him to strike me for talking like that. I didn't want to cry. Crying felt weak, and I was determined not to be weak. For the first time, I felt like I had unzipped the costume I had been wearing and let someone see what was really underneath— an ugly God-hater.

"Danica, I know this sounds crazy... but you need to forgive God."

Her words stopped me. *Forgive God?* I could hardly hear past what I felt like was heresy. She explained it wasn't about dethroning Him or saying He had done wrong. It was about facing the lies I had believed about Him and letting truth replace them. Forgiveness, even toward God, was about my freedom.

That day I left her office confused and raw. Months into the program, I still couldn't believe I was here. Living in a rehab center, watched closely. Monitored even in the quick five-minute showers, because I couldn't stop cutting myself. Feeling like an animal. And me, the "good girl," was the one with the problem.

I remembered our very first meeting. I had walked in ready to challenge her, to see if she could get through my walls. I gave her my whole story like a grocery list: *"Grew up Christian. Loved Jesus. Was abused. Drank. Tried to kill myself. Went to ministry school. Fell away from God. Got mixed up with the wrong people, more drinking, some drugs, another suicide attempt... and now I'm here."*

I thought laying it all out would keep her from digging deeper. But she didn't buy it.

Our sessions stayed on the surface for months. She was also the program director, so sometimes she couldn't meet with me at all, which I took as rejection. I thought counseling was supposed to be someone asking you hard questions, you crying, and then walking out feeling better. But most days, I left feeling nothing at all.

Until that day I told her I was mad at God. Something shifted. I realized I trusted her.

The truth was, I had spent my whole life trying to be the good kid—at least where people could see. Sure, I had messed up here and there. Once, my parents grounded me from my best friend for a year after we got drunk together. But even in rehab, I felt like it was my job to "pastor" everyone else. Which really meant wearing masks to cover my own mess.

That session cracked half those masks. She knew now I didn't trust God, and that most of what I said about Him wasn't what I believed. Admitting it was like tearing down a fortress I had built for years.

Not long after, one of the other counselors encouraged us to write spoken word pieces. I wasn't interested, but I tried anyway. At my next meeting with Mrs. A, I pulled out a wrinkled sheet of paper.

"Who am I really?
Why even know?

Every day is just a show.
If I let my guard down,
Then they'll know that deep inside
I'm just a broken, hurting little girl..."

I finished reading and waited for her to praise the scripture I had woven into it. Instead, she surprised me.

"I can't believe you put that in there," she said.

She read my own words back to me, and the shame was instant. There were things I had pushed so far down I had almost forgotten them, but hearing them aloud felt unbearable.

"Danica, do you want to talk about it yet?" Her question triggered me.

Reluctantly I agreed, but I couldn't say it outloud. That afternoon during quiet time, I began to write. I started at the very beginning and didn't stop. I wrote every memory in detail. The people. The rooms. The smells. The moments my innocence was stolen. I felt the pain and kept going for days.

When I finally read it to her, she looked at me like a mother who had just heard her child's darkest secrets. I felt exposed. Naked. Shame sat heavy on my chest. I wanted to run.

But God was exposing it for a reason. Not to humiliate me, but to show the enemy's schemes for what they were and break them.

It no longer mattered if I could lead the Bible plan for the other girls or be the model student. I was broken. I was desperate. And I needed the power of Jesus.

From that point on, something began to shift. I found

moments of healing. I was held. I was accepted. I learned what it meant to be desperate for Jesus to heal me. I poured more tears on that altar than I ever gave to sleep. And when I laid down the masks and walls, He met me there.

I thought that moment might be the end of the story, like I could sail on out of the program. But it wasn't. God was only getting started and He did so much in me during my year there. I walked out not an addict, but also a stronger believer than I'd ever been.

Chapter 11

The Second Chance

Returning to ministry school was such a crazy idea, and honestly, I still don't know where it came from. But it was one where I felt like the Lord was giving me a chance to finish things, and I had a lot of prophetic words confirming it. So, I wrote letters to the admission team (since I couldn't use email or make calls), and the doors to the school flew open. I was confident in returning and hopeful of being a missionary.

After graduating from rehab in June, I went back to Alabama to get ready for second-year ministry school, almost 4 or 5 years after I had completed the first year. Talk about a weird dynamic. Some teachers had moved on, students were much younger, and I didn't know many people. I also carried a lot of shame walking in the door as an "ex-addict". But I went. The Lord blessed it.

As a second-year student who had been through what felt like hell between my first and second year, I was determined not to let my past define me or restrict me anymore from doing God's work. Though I did battle with carrying

that guilt from time to time. That second year was stretching, and I signed up for my second missions' trip.

Though I had always had dreams of orphanages and
building homes in Africa for many years, it wasn't on the list
of places to go. After hearing the options, I tossed the decision between going to the Philippines and India. I was
getting a little excited for the Philippines when I would look
up photos, but the night before we had to submit our
choices, I had a dream that I was on red soil in a black dress
in a land that looked like Africa. Confused as to why God
would show me Africa when it wasn't a choice, I just
randomly selected India the next morning and went about
my day.

A fun side note worth mentioning though is that little
did I know, two years later I would move to South Asia, be
wearing a black dress, and ask a buddy to take a picture of
me for my Facebook fundraising page. I was so overwhelmed when I looked back at the photo, and it was the
same image that I had seen in that dream before I picked my
second-year mission trip years before. It was just another
example of how beautiful the story God writes can be.

That second year was a picture of redemption for me,
like a second chance that propelled me forward. With every
set back, I grew a little more mature in my desire to be
steadfast and earnest. The Lord began a redemptive thread
in my life and began to use my testimony in platform
ministry classes. We were able to visit rehab centers, and I
had invitations to speak at a couple of rehabs on my own,
too. I shared my story of being like Jonah, who knew the
voice of the Lord but didn't obey and was swallowed up and
then delivered. It was healing to see the Lord thread my life
back together.

It was a strange year, too. As it was a year where I

encountered the Lord in ways I never had before. I spent my personal time in prayer as much as I could and studying the lives of people like AA Allen, Kathryn Kuhlman, and William Branham who loved the glory of the Lord and walked in a powerful anointing. I also attended glory meetings outside of school and had a lot of experiences I couldn't explain. I spent a lot of time praying that year, just on my face in worship before the Lord and began to flow in the prophetic like I had never done before. It was a beautiful season of seeking Him and experiencing the physical manifestations of His presence, which I hadn't quite encountered like that before. I also really started seeing the hand of the Lord move in my life and saw many people around me healed and touched by the Lord.

Mid-year, I got a little distracted by a relationship, but it ended up resolving itself and God protected me. I got a little hurt in the process and backed out of reading the word so much, but I'm thankful for leaders who had insight into this and called me back higher and "slapped me around a little" in a good way.

At that time, I had also been having a lot of issues fundraising, and as soon as I gave God control of the situation that had been distracting me and repented of my sin, the cloud above my head lifted and the weird feeling between me and the Lord ceased. Almost immediately after that, God gave me a financial miracle. I had come to a place where I believed I wouldn't be able to go to India. But miraculously, my India trip was paid off in a day. I was able to then focus on my studies and spend time in the Word and prayer.

The remainder of the year was glorious. A time of God's faithfulness and sweet moments building history with Him.

Chapter 12

The Ache

I could not sleep on the sixteen-hour flight from Dallas to Doha for multiple reasons. It could have been that I was still big enough to need a seatbelt extender, every baby on the plane was crying and screaming, no one seemed to believe in deodorant, or that I simply could not believe I was on my way. But I made it through the three flights and stepped into India—the land I was not, still am not, and may never be "ready" for.

Since my heart was set on Africa and I believed this trip was just another step to prepare me for the door that would eventually open there, I never expected India to grip me the way it did. Before we even stepped off the plane, walking through the jet bridge, you could feel the smothering heat, smell the spices and perspiration, and sense a strange heaviness that clung to the mind. And yet, my heart ached. Physically ached. It was the same deep groaning I had felt years before at that youth camp, lying in my bunk and praying for nations in their own tongues. Back then, when God whispered the word "missionary" over my life, I had no idea where He would send me. Now, standing in the heat and haze of India, I realized I was walking into a chapter He had written long before I knew the plot.

On that trip, our team laughed harder than I think I ever have in my life. If you knew the friends who went with me, you would believe it without question. Together we survived power cuts, tried to order takeout pizza in bad Indian accents, saw strange street dogs, choked on green chilies hidden in every dish, got stuck in an elevator in 120-degree heat, and swore we might actually die from the weather. For anyone considering India, May is not the month to go.

We nearly missed a flight back to the main city where we were staying. One moment we were sprinting through the airport, begging the gate agents to let us in, and the next we were sitting silently, waiting for the pilots to even show up. The food was too spicy, the music was too loud, and the young girls sang off-key, which gave us a headache. But none of those things could overshadow the hunger and desperation for God that we witnessed.

Here I was, nine thousand miles from home, surrounded by people who were literal seekers. At the core of their hearts they wanted to know God and please Him. The hunger was indescribable and greater than anything I had ever seen in the Western church. They would fast for days, walk miles to get to church, and risk being cut off from their families. They were willing to pay the price for the presence of Jesus, a price I had rarely considered in my own faith.

We gathered testimonies from believers who had left everything to follow Christ. For them, faith was not about being a "good person" or building a respectable life. In fact, following Jesus meant losing their influence, their security, and often the approval of their loved ones. They were in it for Christ and Christ alone. Many of them lived the reality that "draw near to God, and He will draw near to you." And He did. His presence met us in every prayer meeting, every service, every whispered worship song.

I had seen miracles in the United States, but what I saw here felt different. I will never forget the first time God used me to minister healing to a little girl. We were teaching in a worship school when she came to me, unable to hear well because of a large boil growing inside her ear. It protruded so much I could feel it through her hair. My team was praying with someone else, so I laid my hands on her and prayed a simple prayer. She went back to playing, and I thought nothing of it. Later, she came running back. The boil was gone, and she could hear perfectly.

We saw many give their lives to Jesus, prayed with countless people, and experienced the Lord's presence in ways that left us speechless. I can still remember the cold marble floors where we sat to pray, the rooftop where we watched the sun rise, and the terrace that looked over the neighborhood. Those moments felt like small altars built in my heart. And as I think back, I realize they were not isolated memories but another thread in the same story God had been weaving all along—a story that started with a teenage girl praying for unknown faces and nations, and continued here, in the heat and dust of India, where the faces finally had names. It was so special.

Chapter 13

The Ministry

After that trip was over, I signed up for an internship with a missions organization and moved away to Tennessee for nine months to train and prepare to move overseas for a year. South Asia was now in the mix because of my recent trip to India, though I also considered other places like Russia or Africa. The idea of choosing anywhere in the world felt overwhelming at times, but my heart kept circling back to India. Even my friends would tell me to stop pretending it would be anywhere else. Africa was mostly children's ministry, and while I loved children, my heart knew that my calling was somewhere else. God had already gripped me too tightly for South Asia.

So I trained. We studied culture, language, and the history of missions. We prepared our bodies for the demands of the field, practiced preaching and teaching, learned how to support and sustain ministry work, and spent hours in prayer. We hiked in the Smoky Mountains, not just for fitness, but to understand perseverance. I laminated missionary training guides knowing they'd end up in places I'd probably never see, and I treated that work like it mattered—because it did.

The Lord was shaping me in ways I didn't fully see at the time. He was teaching me to hear His voice more clearly, to walk in obedience, and to trust Him in the small things so I'd trust Him in the big ones. And on June 6th—exactly two years after I had walked into rehab with my head as low as it could go—I stepped onto a plane bound for South Asia as a commissioned missionary, redeemed from my past.

Operating under God's anointing was like nothing else in the world. It was holy, humbling, and so alive with purpose that there were moments I forgot the cost entirely. But there were also moments that pushed me to my physical limits—like the time I went to get a plate of rice after a baby's first birthday party and ended up laying hands on over 500 people until someone finally intercepted me so I could eat.

I learned quickly that life on the field was both breathtaking and exhausting. Once, while hosting a visiting team, I jumped off a train to tease my local contact, Aruna, thinking I had more than two minutes to get back on. The train left me—shocking us both—and I'll never forget her screaming my name as I ran as fast as I could to catch it. Another time, I started walking 14 kilometers a day so I could pray for our pastors who made the same trek to their village churches, sometimes facing snake bites or beatings from radicals along the way. I wanted to know what their journey felt like. And one afternoon in the city, that walk brought me face to face with a puffed-up king cobra, ready to strike. I froze, remembering something I'd read about them being able to spit venom and blind people—or kill an African elephant. I wasn't that big, but I still didn't like my odds. I prayed in the

Holy Spirit, and just like that, it slithered back over the log, completely uninterested in me. I kept walking, though with a lot more praying than walking that day.

Not every challenge was spiritual—some were just miserable. Like the time I thought I had dengue fever and the local doctors were convinced I might die. They made me eat papaya every day for two weeks, and to this day, even the smell of it makes me gag. But the Lord kept me, over and over.

Life became a rhythm of preaching, praying, worshiping, planting churches, sharing songs in slum communities, teaching in the ministry school, hosting teams, traveling to new cities, interceding late into the night, and watching God set people free. I saw girls arrive to us possessed and leave as leaders in the church, bringing others into the kingdom. I saw hundreds lift their hands to receive Jesus and many more filled with the Holy Spirit. And somewhere along the way, the culture I once entered as a foreigner began to feel like home.

Though my time as a full-time missionary was short—wrapping up in under three years—the impact of those days is still with me. I really felt like I was thriving and excelling in my work.

But sadly, something began to happen.

Chapter 14

The Deviation

I did not drift all at once. At first, it was little things I could brush aside. A lingering heaviness that clung to me even after ministry trips. A tiredness I could not sleep away. Moments when the joy I had known so deeply felt just out of reach. But the longer I pressed forward without stopping to realign my heart, the further I strayed from the place God had called me to be.

That is the thing about drifting. It is rarely dramatic at first. It is subtle. You are still moving forward, still thinking you are on course, until one day you look up and realize you are miles from where you were meant to be.

When a pilot is flying an airplane, they have countless instruments, switches, and tools to help them navigate from one destination to another. You have probably seen pictures of a cockpit before. At first glance, all those dials and gauges can look overwhelming. But once a pilot is trained in how each one works, they can use them to chart a safe and accurate path through the sky.

One of the first instruments student pilots learn to use is the directional gyro, or heading indicator. It looks like a compass, showing directional degrees. For example, 090 degrees is true east. Technically, 091 is still east, but if you keep turning without correction, soon you are heading 120 degrees, a clear shift toward the southeast.

When a pilot plans a flight from Dallas to Los Angeles, they follow a specific heading. During the journey, they must use both the heading indicator and the magnetic compass. The heading indicator is smooth and stable but drifts over time. The magnetic compass is tied to the Earth's magnetic field but can be momentarily thrown off. Pilots are trained to continually check and align the two, making regular corrections to stay on course.

Even on a short flight, a five-degree deviation might not seem like much. You are still going east, right? But over time, those five degrees will put you more than a hundred miles off course.

This is exactly what happened to me, both on the mission field and in my spiritual life. I cannot point to the exact moment I started to drift. It was not intentional. It was not malicious. But over time, fear, doubt, compromise, and sheer exhaustion began to pull me off my original heading.

Living in a foreign country, navigating multiple cultures and languages, and facing constant spiritual pressure was not easy. I had faced persecution, threats, and the reality of being a foreigner in a land where my faith was often viewed as dangerous. Friends and brothers in Christ were chased, beaten, stalked, and persecuted because of their faith. I prayed with my eyes open, always aware of who might be coming for me next, unnecessary fear set in. I avoided immigration officials, quietly altered my reasons for being there to keep my visa safe, and felt the weight of spiritual opposition pressing in.

The enemy will use anything to get your eyes off Jesus.

If he cannot pull you away through outright sin, he will try distraction, discouragement, or even the weight of success. If he can shift your focus from the One who called you to the waves around you, he knows you will start to sink.

Like Peter, I had once stepped out of the boat in faith, walking on water. But now the waves looked bigger than the One who had called me.

There were practical struggles too. Days without water or power. A support budget so low I often had to choose between one need and another. Deep loneliness without a team beside me. The idols in the streets seemed to tower over the invisible God I preached about. While my earlier seasons with the Lord had dug deep wells in my spirit, I was no longer drawing fresh water. I was living off yesterday's oil. Without daily realignment, my course kept shifting, and I did not notice until I was far from center.

Yet God's mercy held me. I never renounced my faith, and I was not living in blatant sin. Like David in the Psalms, I prayed earnestly, loved Jesus deeply, but could not seem to shake fear, doubt, and compromise. Outwardly, ministry went on. Villages lined up for prayer. The power of God would fall. Miracles still happened. Signs and wonders still followed. But inwardly, I was weary and worn.

I was nine thousand miles from home, poor, needy, lonely, and aching inside. My dependence on God and my history with Him carried me for a time, but the cracks were forming. Little compromises crept in. Small decisions that dulled my sensitivity to the Spirit.

The saddest part of my story was not persecution, heartbreak, or even personal loss. It was losing my consecration. Nothing compares to realizing that the sweet, tangible anointing you once carried has lifted because you allowed yourself to drift.

I noticed it when the demons stopped coming out of people, when the lies sounded louder than truth, when blind eyes stopped opening, when support dried up, and when ministry shifted from being my calling to being my occupation. I was good at it, but that was all it had become.

It is possible to be successful in ministry while slowly dying inside. You can still preach, still pray for people, still see fruit, but if your own heart is compromised, you will eventually run dry.

Like Peter, I lost sight of Jesus while still out on the water. And instead of crying out for Him to save me, I sank.

But praise be to God, even in the next five dark years, Jesus never let me drown.

Chapter 15

The "Normal Life"

When I came home from the field, I was so worn out and hurt that I told myself I just wanted a normal life. I'd been "marked by God" my whole life, always surrounded by His mercy. I just wanted to forget the yet once again squandered call on my life. I was lonely and spent. And I'd dedicated years now to preaching, traveling, sacrificing, and walking in what seemed like radical obedience, as per my thinking. I poured out my life, all of my heart for both this God and a nation, but I was exhausted and not just physically, but spiritually and emotionally too. Beneath all the fire I had for the Lord was a slow-burning disillusionment I didn't yet have language for. I told myself I just needed to rest. Regroup. Settle into a life that didn't demand miracles for survival. I had survived the mission field alone with no spouse, no team, no support. Now was my time to find someone, anyone, to keep me from doing life alone. I had a void, and I was determined to fill it.

Technically, I was still on furlough. My missions debrief hadn't taken place yet, though I had an idea of what my leaders would have planned for me. While I waited for that debrief to happen, the weeks were long and I had already moved back to my hometown, taken a job, and started rebuilding something that looked like stability, though it was still insecure. That's when I met my husband.

We met online. It was unexpected and fast. Really, I was not planning to meet him or anyone that way. But when all the girls at the office were on a dating site and comparing their matches during lunch hour, I gave in when they tempted me to try it. I agreed to *try it*, but just for one weekend to see what happened. Who knew that very first swipe would be an Indian man? Alabama didn't really have a big Indian population or community, especially where I was from. What were the odds? So, I swiped, honestly curious in him, but I was not even sure how the app worked. Hearts popped up, we'd matched.

Adrenaline pumped through me when he messaged me, asking me out the same day. That adrenaline continued as things moved quickly, and within weeks, really, I decided to marry him. He seemed good. Loyal. Stable. Kind. He was full of potential to give me the life I sought after. I hadn't told my leaders. I didn't really tell my friends. It was crazy, I knew it was crazy. But somehow, this just made sense.

But on the other hand, everything about the relationship, especially by traditional ministry standards, looked like it shouldn't work, and shouldn't have. He was Hindu. From another country. A different culture. He didn't understand my culture, and I didn't fully understand his. My parents would die. Shoot, his parents would *really* die. But somehow, he felt safe. This stranger...safe? Safe like still water, I could predict the future with him.

With him, I didn't have to be a leader. I didn't have to be intense or watch my convictions. I didn't have to always be on fire. I could rest. I could have a normal life. And at least if I had lost all purpose and identity, I could be married and have kids.

He didn't propose with a ring, but we later got one, and it was and still is so beautiful. He wasn't overly emotional like I wanted, but he was steadfast in his commitment to marrying me. We didn't plan a perfect ceremony. It was all fast and quiet. In fact, our actual marriage happened by accident. Truly.

We were coming back from my birthday trip, which we had taken to Knoxville, where we had also just gotten my ring and taken engagement photos. He wanted to stop by the courthouse to ask about the marriage license instead of looking it up online. It felt like the right thing to do since neither of us had been married before, and we didn't even know the process with immigration. Honestly, we thought we were just asking our questions. But the next thing I knew, we were following a volunteer minister through a doorway and standing under an artificial flower arch at the county courthouse. No rings. No witnesses. Just a quick questioning glance at each other, a couple of tears, and a yes.

I remember looking at him right before the vows and asking, "Are we really doing this?" He looked at me calmly and solidly and said, "I am ready if you are." And that was it.

It was an exciting moment of built tension followed by a quick doubt and then sudden relief. It wasn't just that I was in love; it was that love gave me a break from the pressure of my calling. I could be human. And that felt holy. That felt real after a world of putting on a show to maintain monthly support.

We began our life quietly, and honestly, it worked. We worked hard and had a lot of sweet moments together in those first days. The business we managed together hadn't quite grown to the place it would yet, and we lived without work pressure. We had a lot of fun in those beginning days, the lingering honeymoon effects, both surprised that "fate" had brought us together.

We weren't sure of what life would look like, but we knew we wanted a baby right away. Sadly, as many others also face some issues, we also struggled to get pregnant for over a year. That initial longing for a child was brutal. But later, and miraculously, we were blessed with our daughter. She was the light of our lives. There were struggles, of course—losses, cultural differences, arguments—but we had joy. The first eighteen months of her life were so beautiful. We were so happy. A few arguments happened here and there, but it was all normal stuff, and we always made it through. We even started traveling, waltzing our baby girl throughout Europe, having the time of our lives. I still look back with great joy.

Then came the move to Dallas. A place I'd actually grown fond of and had wanted to move to, but I wanted to make that decision myself, not the way it ended up happening.

Instead, right at Thanksgiving, we left Alabama thinking we were coming for a temporary work assignment to help develop a new department within our company.

But we never came home.

Chapter 16

The Shock

The morning that we left to go to Dallas for our two-month assignment, I took a pregnancy test. Positive. I knew immediately it was a boy. I was so happy. There was this unexplainable knowing. Life was growing inside me again. It felt like a fresh start.

When we arrived in Dallas, we temporarily enrolled my daughter in a cute little day school. It was so precious seeing her surrounded with other little Indian babies in her community. Something we didn't have back home. As for the new pregnancy though, I'm not exaggerating even a little when I tell you that it was terrible for me in the first trimester. It's usually hard for everyone, but I could barely function, and I was sent to the city on business. I was very sick and anemic and couldn't focus. But I was trying. My husband and I were already on edge from the stress of it all, but still, we kept going.

Then one day after the holidays, I got the text. My brother said our dad had gone to the hospital via ambulance after a fall. My husband jokingly told me the text said he was dying, so I jumped up to grab my phone. But when I read it, it didn't say that. Still, I had a bad feeling.

As the news got progressively worse from the time he arrived at the hospital that day, within 24 hours, I was on a plane back to Birmingham. The fall had revealed more than we expected.

We knew he wasn't doing perfectly. But lab results showed he had a UTI, which led to a full-body infection, which led to paralysis. Yes, seriously. Then a stroke. What?! Then a coma. The man who had taught me to love the Lord, who had sent me to the nations, who had pastored our family, was unconscious, and his body was shutting down. Before our eyes, we saw what can never be fully described.

To get rid of the infection that was eating his body, they removed part of his spine to try to isolate it. He was on life support, and they gave us very little hope. When I saw him that night after coming off the plane, and he had just gotten out of surgery, my knees buckled. As the doctor explained how the operation went, I couldn't even hear what was being said. I just sat there, looking at my dad, who didn't even look human anymore. He was swollen, yellow, and purple—covered in braces, wires, and everything was bandaged and taped up.

But we believed. We had faith. After all, we served God. My dad was a fighter. A believer. A preacher even. We laid hands. We worshiped. We rallied our people. And slowly, he started responding! It was a miracle. He moved. He talked. He couldn't walk, but he could feel something as he wiggled his toes even one day later. I flew back to Dallas thinking we were in the clear. He was going to make it. Everything was going to be okay. Maybe God was still in the healing business!

My mission to my job continued, and normal life resumed as best as it could. We went all in on our work project. But the pregnancy utilized all the iron I had left in my body. I tried to recover from the severe nausea and critical anemia that had me literally passing out in grocery stores. Really, y'all, it was bad. One time, I pushed myself to make it to the pharmacy inside Target because I knew I was about to collapse. I woke up in the shampoo aisle to my 2-year-old crying after seeing my fall. I was so scared; I thought they were going to take me to jail and take my daughter away from me. I was sick.

Chapter 17

The Unraveling

I was completely depleted from all the ups and downs with my dad and not being able to be there with him or fully explain why I couldn't be there. I couldn't even go out in public or be a good mom. My husband took up my extra work to help me on top of everything else he had to take care of, and slowly, tension came within our marriage. My life grew increasingly complicated. But I had hope for my dad. And early on, I officially found out I was having a boy. I wanted to tell my dad. I wanted him to hold on for that moment—to meet his grandson. His first grandson after three granddaughters.

Within me was a little boy who could ride tractors and four-wheelers, rope cows, ride horses, go fishing, and do all the things. I saw it clearly, my childhood experiences for my kid, but a thousand times better because he'd be an actual boy and have the freedom to do all those fun, rugged things. Right after I found out, I called my brother and asked him to put the phone to dad's ear, and I told him it was a boy. They told me Dad was happy, but he still couldn't really respond. Still, it was good news worth holding on for.

This whole recovery process lasted for what seemed like forever; it did last for months. He got better, we were so relieved, and we gladly moved him to a recovery rehab hospital. We were full of faith. But something shifted, and we still don't know why. After he started really recovering, it was like he just let go completely. I think that when he realized he'd likely never walk again, he decided he wouldn't really be able to live. He asked to change his status to "do not resuscitate," and he clarified his living will. He was coherent just enough, and he asked to go home to hospice.

My brother and I were stunned. How could hospice even be a discussion for us at this point in our lives? We were so reluctant, but due to some other conditions, doctors told us it could be hours before he was gone. As we prepared to take him home, they wanted to prepare us that he needed constant monitoring and medication, and he wouldn't have a lot of time.

With that in mind and us not being ready to let go, we challenged his decision with such grief. The whole situation was so unfair. How could this be happening? And for the love of God, why did I pass out (like completely lose consciousness) every day during this pregnancy?! We begged him not to give up. But we could see what happened and reluctantly brought him home. That's when the night-mare continued.

Prepared for hours, we had twelve torturous days. Really, the worst twelve days someone could live through, even though there were moments here and there that were beautiful.

But in the end, hospice can be so cruel, as it's the gateway to death. It's hard. It's sad. It is a blessing, but it's so very painful. Anyone who says it's peaceful has not lived it in the room. And if you're going through that or have—I'm so sorry.

We watched our precious dad slip in and out of awareness. We watched him forget who we were, then remember again. We watched him fight demons in his sleep. He cried. He got angry. He refused to eat and then needed his comfort measures more. We watched visitors come and go, singing his praises, bringing food, holding hands, and then walking out the door. And we stayed. My brother was there more than I was because I was still so sick that I could barely stand up. And that guilt on the drive back home to my empty apartment felt so incredibly heavy. My baby was back in Texas; my husband was still carrying both his and my workload so he was always at the office. I was left to deal with this heartbreak alone, and once again felt misunderstood.

The only thing I feel I successfully did in those twelve days was gain weight, because the only thing we could control was eating something that felt good. And in the south, they're gonna bring food. I cried in silence. I stopped talking. I stopped hoping. We were all beyond tired. And I felt utterly alone. I was so overwhelmed with emotions with everything going on, I couldn't even think about what was happening to me or in my life.

Due to the strain of it all, my husband and I were still having a hard time in our marriage, and in the last three days of my dad's life, I sat alone, broken as deeply as I could be, as my dad literally died. Years later, I still can't quite explain the feeling. There was no one to hug me. No one to tell me they were praying for me. No one to cry to. And I couldn't think about anything.

I couldn't think about inheritance; I couldn't think about the funeral. I was alone in every possible way. My mother had remarried. My brother had his own family, and losing my dad and walking through that last season brought its own hardships to him. My daughter was back in Texas, and gosh, my poor baby was away from her parents. I hoped she didn't feel abandoned. It also stung because I moved away when I was 17, and no one knew me enough to even mention me at the funeral when they spoke, and all the stories and condolences went to my brother. Since all this was too much, it felt as if I didn't exist and was an illegitimate child.

That final day my dad was with us in hospice, I mustered up the courage to talk to my dad. I sat beside his bed, held his hand, kissed his forehead, and told him I loved him. I told him it was okay to go. And I meant it. I also told him that I would be okay, and he must've been so close to eternity at that point to know that would end up being true. Because in that moment, I was not okay, and I was too tired to ask him to stay. But how could I ask anyone to stay in such a painful and cruel world? My confidence in the way of life was fading. After that small piece, I couldn't bear to say another word, and I left the room, afraid to be with my own dad as he died.

I knew that he'd be going soon, and I anticipated it to happen quickly, as if his last breath would free me. I had no idea it would only get worse. Absolutely exhausted, I came back into the room and I laid down on the couch behind his head. I glanced at him and quickly looked away, fighting tears as I watched my dad struggle to breathe. His body frail and unable to go on. I laid there for only a few seconds while I was just waiting for someone to "rip the Band-Aid off" to end this nightmare.

As I laid down to rest, my sister-in-law sat next to his

bed. I honestly think my dad saw us all settle—finally, and within seconds, he exhaled.

One last breath.

And then he was gone. I couldn't believe it. My heart shattered, but I remained silent. Everyone clung to his lifeless body. It felt like I wasn't even in the room anymore, I just watched and cried as my whole world collapsed within me.

That final breath he took also took a piece of me with it. Honestly, many pieces. I didn't just lose my father. I lost my compass. My anchor. My sense of being held. There was no longer a backup plan for me if my life went south. No one to call if I had a question about my car, no one to call if I needed an answer to any question in life. Who else would tell me the difference between a Phillips head and a flathead screwdriver, or a 1x4 or 2x6 piece of wood? No one else told me what the lights on in my car meant or what a quick way to make some money was. My dad had always been my locked in security, whether I spent every moment with him or not.

Immediately following the funeral, my husband and I packed our life and apartment in silence and drove the full U-Haul back to Dallas. I left my home state the day after I buried my dad. As if it couldn't possibly be more, my life continued to spiral. When I came back to Dallas, I felt like a ghost of myself, a proper shell of a human. I wasn't angry at God, I just didn't know what to believe anymore. Doubt entered in, and the pain was too much. The silence was too much. The pressure to bounce back was too much. And I was pregnant and sick, trying to manage life with a toddler whose mom had just abandoned her for weeks.

So, I stopped trying to be anything. And I just started to react to all the problems. I was told I had pregnancy complications that could end badly. And then, when that was resolved, I was told the baby would be breeched. Then, when he turned around, I still had to have an emergency c-section because the cord had wrapped around his neck, and they lost his heart rate completely. I was so tired of wavering hope and believing things could be better. My life seemed to attract bad news and unpleasant circumstances time after time. I was starting to believe in karma.

Because of the emergency c-section, I quickly asked for something to calm my anxiety. The anesthesiologist saw my nerves were tattered and gave me something very strong. In fact, I was so drugged, I don't remember my entire stay at the hospital with the baby. I only remembered a few things, and after all this had happened, my husband drove me home from the hospital.

Freshly cut open, and not sure how to care for such a tiny baby after losing so much blood in the operation, I was nervous for my husband to even leave me to take a shower alone. It was at that point that I hit my bottom. I was helpless.

I hated that I had just birthed a baby to come and live in my mess. I felt so guilty about being his mom and over-whelmed that my little girl was staying at a friend's house for that first night.

Chapter 18

The Fade

In that season of being overwhelmed, things grew increasingly hard, and I'd grown comfortable in compromising my faith. Years had passed since I had lived in South Asia, and the heartbreak of losing my dad on top of my marriage feeling insecure left me unstable. Though I had always had certain parameters that I was never willing to cross because of my upbringing, I still began opening my heart to religious curiosity. After seeing others deconstruct and open their minds to other things and seeing them appear happier, I also "took charge of my life" and got an energy healer to support me in that dark time. I needed her, since no one else was there. I loved her so much (and still do—but she ended up getting fired) and I loved our sessions. My spirit guides always had so much to say, and she made me feel so supported and loved unlike everyone else in my life. I finally felt seen and heard.

I felt iffy about my choice, but I justified it because I still quoted Scripture, but I also started talking about "Source." I still said I followed Jesus, but I started burning incense, listening to teachings on energy, praying to the universe. Doing breathwork, following eastern practices and repeating mantras started feeling like a good thing. I felt like I was getting wiser as my mind opened.

Before I knew it, I was living out Romans Chapter 1:21-23.

"Because, although they knew God, they did not glorify Him as God, nor were thankful, but became futile in their thoughts, and their foolish hearts were darkened. Professing to be wise, they became fools, and changed the glory of the incorruptible God into an image made like corruptible man—and birds and four-footed animals and creeping things."

Though I once knew and walked with God, I began to grow particularly fond of specific gods and idols that had specific purposes. I even began tattooing symbols that represented those gods on my body. I loved Buddha, who brought me peace. I liked the Hindu god, Ganesha, who removed my obstacles and was a cute little elephant guy with a friendly rat. It seemed very harmless. And then of course there was Lakshmi, who gave fertility and wealth. It was all good things; I began to justify. Blending the cultures gave me breathing room. I told myself it was wisdom. Maturity. Growth. It all became true for me.

I wanted peace. I wanted control. I wanted to survive, and I was so desperate to do whatever that took—except what had proven to work for me before. I was deep enough down the rabbit hole, that coming back up would require deep humility and I couldn't do it.

All this new life looked good. It felt right, it made me feel better and in control of myself. I was living in tune with my body, which helped me process my grief which was still so very heavy. I was "raising my vibration." I was talking about "alignment" and "healing my inner child." I read books that talked about Jesus and Buddha. The further I went, the more everything made sense. Even Allah had some truth to it, so I thought. It was all leading to the same place.

My spiritual curiosity made me feel more mature and at peace with humanity. The black and white lines I once honored had merged to grey and less conviction filled my heart, which in turn comforted me when I lived outside of what I knew to be the will of God.

Though I knew I was wrong, I wasn't looking to be defiant or go against Jesus or what I had always known. I was only seeking to be open wanting to ensure I left no stone unturned. I never fully committed to one practice over another, but I had no idea this also made me not committed to Jesus at all. Sure, there would be a worship song in the background on rare occasions, and I'd feel a goosebump or two. I even remember some moments where I got a good cry. I'd throw up a random prayer to Jesus when I had some trouble and Jesus was still my default deity, though I was slowly training myself to find alternates.

When I would have a hard time, and that season post-partum was full of hard times, I would (just like the Hindus) spend my days conducting puja and visiting priests, asking them to pray that my husband would love me again. I'd also write letters to my inner child or seek guidance from the spirits. My Indian friends complimented me on my dedication to their culture and gods. My kids started seeing these idols as their own gods.

Becoming my highest self, I felt myself rising out of the darkness with all the counterfeit things I had begun to do in my life to restore my faith. I felt the gradual rise again and felt my practices were working. I had a solution, a good one. I didn't have to constrain myself to serve a God I couldn't see. I could have whatever god I wanted, or even better, be my own god. Practicing universalism, raising myself up to where I was always meant to be, manifesting the life I dreamed of all whiles honoring all cultures and religions—it was a slow fade from curious to "sure." I was a universalist.

Things were suddenly going great, amid outward turmoil. Then the unimaginable happened.

Chapter 19

The Party Before the Plunge

It's not unheard of for Indians who live in the west to send their children back to India to be raised by their grandparents for a season. And though I honored that as part of their culture, I had always said no when it came to my own children. I always had a stance that if I needed someone else to raise them, God wouldn't have given them to me. But after a long fight with cultural norms and pressure in my workplace grew to give it my all, I struggled with the choice that felt more like a commandment. Finally, realizing this would give me time to heal and work hard, and a better life for the kids when they came home, I reluctantly agreed.

When my baby boy was only 8 months old, I sent him 9000 miles away to India to live for a while. That's what being a good mom looked like, that's how I would be able to do it all. It was very sad, but my son was fine. He enjoyed the culture, and it was great for my in-laws to get to spend time with him. Shortly after, I also sent my daughter so she could become bilingual. With my children gone away from me, I had truly nothing.

I missed my kids more than I ever thought possible. I quickly realized that what I had done to make their lives, and our lives better was a sacrifice I wasn't sure I could recover from. It was my heart on the altar. I mean sure, I could FaceTime them, but babies can't express how they're doing, and twelve and a half hours' time difference made it extremely hard to make a connection. My son began to see my mother-in-law as his mom, and my daughter had been abandoned, going from relative to relative in multiple cities in a country far from her own. I was overcome with guilt, but my friends and family from India were all fine with our decision to leave them there. After all, I could work hard, bringing extra income which in turn supported their future. We could make and save money all the while our kids could learn about their other culture and language and be raised by someone who had proven at raising an Indian kid. It was a win-win-win set up even though I felt I had lost.

In this season, I utilized the newly found free time for self gain, and I silenced the voice of reasoning and abandoned my faith all together. I exchanged the truth of God for a lie, was bound in idolatry and the remainder of Romans 1 became true for me. I became someone else. I thought differently and I spoke differently. I dressed differently. The vile things I did had once repulsed me, but now I celebrated them. I was having fun, with an end in sight. I knew I'd get my children back eventually, but until then, I'd have a blast. And now, with nothing on the line, the only one left in my life to be pleased by me was me. I was the boss.

I don't glory in sin, so we don't have to elaborate, but it was dumb. Though it felt like a blast for those few months, it was just pulling me closer to hell. I'd become quite social, partied and did things unbecoming of someone. I seemed like I was good, but I was gradually getting worse.

That facade of happiness and freedom was weak, and the hollowness in my heart lingered. Though all the problems in my marriage seemed restored due to my newfound open mind. As cycles usually go, another fight happened. I couldn't keep it up this time. The fight was smaller than other fights we'd had in the past, but it was the gateway into a depth of emotions I'd buried and buried into the depths.

This time, I couldn't take one more person being disappointed in me, and the very thought my husband was angry with something I'd done had me ready to disappear once and for all. The weight of my sin weighed heavy on me. I had nothing to live for except myself. And I wasn't all that great.

That's when it happened. That's when I took those sleeping pills. That's when I died.

Chapter 20

The Awakening

While it's hard to believe it wasn't sooner, two weeks after that dreadful day in the ER was the true turning point for my life. I resumed life as best as I could and went to Florida and visited with a friend for her birthday. We were at a toss-up over what was the best thing for us to do to celebrate. We tossed around ideas for hours, but thankfully, the good old worldwide web gave us plenty of options. We both had big eyes and excitement when she read the description for a yoga retreat as opposed to some of the other options. But it was not just any yoga retreat. No way, we were the wild ones—we weren't going to spend her birthday in a basic tree pose. We were going to be *awakened*.... we were going to the Kundalini 'awakening' retreat.

Now, if you're unfamiliar with Kundalini, let me give you the rundown. In Hinduism, it's believed to be a spiritual energy coiled at the base of your spine, like a serpent. Through breath-work, chanting, and movement, you try to awaken this energy to achieve higher consciousness. It's become trendy in the West, which is how we found it on a random Saturday night.

By this time, after the incident, I finally felt like I was going to be okay. I still had some lingering issues with my speech and with some heart-related things caused by the lethal dose of the medication I took. I was also left with severe and sporadic anxiety attacks, but I was starting to gain some clarity, and even sparks of joy again, here and there. This opportunity seemed to be right on time, and I felt good about it. I even screamed to my friend in excitement, "Oh man, this must be legit. I just felt led to buy a new journal right before I came here!" I had no idea why I'd need that journal, and it was way better than Kundalini.

I went because I wanted to be awakened. To reach my highest self. After all, that's what I had been seeking all this time. I was all in. I mean, for crying out loud, I had just conquered death. We were both shaking in the car before we walked in, nerves and excitement filled our bodies. Recounting our previous spiritual encounters we'd had together back in ministry school, and how now that we saw the scientific reasoning behind things, it could *all* be real. We finally got out and walked into the room.

When my friend went to the bathroom, I eagerly sat in the first mat position, assuming I'd be the first to receive my awakening. I was excited, ready. I brewed some jasmine tea and let the scent fill the air. I looked around the room, antic-ipation building inside me. I knew, deep down, that my life was about to change. There was an expectancy in my spirit like in times past, it felt like that feeling you get before you answer an altar call. That was further validation for me, this was real. I had no idea just how much my life would change from that night. Way different than I thought.

Before the session started, a girl (one of the facilitators) stood up to share. She was so sweet and seemed so kind and grounded. I listened excitedly and in anticipation. Then I was a little shocked as she continued because she hit a little too close to home. I was all in when she was talking about higher vibrations, light, and love. Then she did something a little weird, and my stomach felt a little uneasy, but I ignored it. That was just my upbringing religion flaring up.

She started talking about "the language of light." She said it was an unknown tongue, glossolalia, the scientists call it, and she explained that sometimes when she prayed, she still used it. She claimed it was speaking in tongues—but not exactly like in the Bible. She said it could be explained scientifically and that it manifests differently depending on who or what you pray to. She said some people pray to Jesus, others to Source, and some to themselves. For her, she got her language of light from the Holy Spirit, she said. Now I want to note here that in the life I was living, though I was trying to be better since the suicide attempt, I didn't really claim to be like the Holy Spirit's greatest fan at that time. But even though I wasn't fully right in the head, I still knew that I didn't fully buy that the Holy Ghost was approving those prayers.

It was weird, and I didn't love it. I started being a little more critical in my mind as I listened to them teach. It was bizarre to me because five minutes before I walked into that room, no one could talk me out of love and light, and that all roads lead to one place. But when she started talking about the Holy Ghost, I knew deep down that Jesus wasn't really in the same company as these other gods and ideas. I felt a little odd, but I had come there for ultimate enlightenment, and I was determined. I wanted to challenge all my beliefs. I wanted to heal from my past. So, despite that little nudge, I stayed open and pushed passed the uncomfortable feeling.

How else would I become enlightened? Openness was what I'd trained myself to do.

The retreat shifted then shifted into a time of "interpretive dancing". Now listen. If you know me at all, in any world and in any capacity, you're already laughing. Because you know that if I start dancing at all, y'all better run, cause something ain't right. Really and truly, I've downed entire bottles of liquor and never even bopped my head. I'm not a dancer. So, I didn't know what to do. The lights were dim. People were literally slithering like snakes. What creeps, I thought. Others moved in whatever way their body "told" them to. I just lightly swayed in anticipation for that to stop at all costs, and then another guy got up and started speaking. That's when I then wished the dancing would have just kept going because I was ready to be a freaking ballerina before we went into what was next.

I remember one of the facilitators who was "laying hands" on people and awakening them was praying to some god; he didn't specify who. But here's the thing: the language he used? It was far from Light. The moment he opened his mouth, I felt it. As the roaring, screeching, gibberish came from his mouth, I felt it so deeply. Something dark. Heavy. My mind flashed back quickly to a time when I was trying to cast out a demon in someone back in India years before. That was a weird flashback, but God, it felt the same.

I pushed myself to stay in the experience, but I couldn't shake it. It sounded like he was speaking Parsel-tongue from Harry Potter. I joked to my friend, "He sounds like he's talking to a snake."

But I wasn't really joking. It was evil.

As he prayed louder and walked closer to me, I started to feel it in my chest. Everything felt tight. The anxiety.

The fear. The weight of something demonic. My breathing changed. My heart pounded. The same feeling I had in the hospital weeks earlier, when I went into SVT before cardiac arrest, I felt again. My heart raced and raced out of control, and I thought I might actually have a heart attack. This was supposed to be peaceful. But I felt unclean. I felt the weight of everything I'd done in the last six months of my life. It was heavier than I could hold. He was getting closer to me now and coming down the row person by person towards me. As I heard his voice grow in volume and felt him close, reality hit me like a ton of bricks. I was so evidently lost, and I hadn't even seen it coming. *I did not belong in that room. I needed help. Real help.*

Without thinking, I clutched my chest and yelled: "HOLY SPIRIT, PROTECT ME!" It escaped from me like a startled scream when someone jumps out from behind a door and says "boo!". The reality of my situation was so weighty. So shocking. I hadn't even admitted to being a universalist until that very day. The deception of trying to be right and sound right without a label, but just a philosophy. What the heck was I doing?! I was not only living outside of a calling. I was walking contrary to who I was. I just laid there for the rest of the night, so confused and twisted, praying those facilitators would either come fast and awaken me or stay the heck away from me.

As I laid there, it struck me that when I cried out, I didn't say "source." I didn't say 'light.' I didn't say "energy." I cried out to Jesus. In my heart, I had said *Spirit of the Living God*, help me right now, or I am going to hell. It was urgent. It was necessary. And somewhere, buried under those layers of confusion and compromise, I knew who was real. I called upon His name.

"For "whoever calls on the name of the LORD *shall be
saved."' Romans* 10:13

The moment I said His name, I knew I didn't belong
there. I knew what I had opened. And I knew I couldn't
keep going. I didn't need to be my highest self, I needed the
Greater One. I needed the *Name above All other names*
working in me. I was shaken awake in that moment. It was
like running towards a first love you should have never left.

Even though I should have, I couldn't get up right then
and there, I was far too polite for that, and I didn't want to
make it awkward for my friend. But for some reason, no one
even really touched me that night. That parsel-tongue guy
kept walking towards me but kept turning sharply when he
would get too close. Another girl came and tried to pray in
what sounded like elvish over me and touched my forehead
for less than a second and disappeared. Deep down, I knew
the Lord had answered my prayer. He protected me from
further damage.

After the experience, my friend and I quickly debriefed
in the car, and I told her I felt unsettled and needed to go
somewhere safe. That language was even weird to me, and
I'm sure it even took her off guard. I didn't know how to
adequately describe what had just happened to me, because
from the looks and sounds of it, she had appeared to have
the best night of her life. Meanwhile, two feet away from
her, I was fighting literal hell.

Even though it was late after the kundalini experience, I
was so rattled that I couldn't go back home yet, and we went
out to the pier and overlooked the moon reflecting off the
water. But the December wind was too chilly, so we
grabbed a pizza and went home.

Overcome by the whole experience, I had some aid in

going to sleep and passed out. I thought the edible would've made things normal again but the next morning, I couldn't just sit there and chat. I woke up early, went out to the beach, and began to journal and reflect. I did a couple of meditations, searched some numerology, and looked for signs from the universe of what happened to me. But it wasn't resonating with me as deeply as it had before and I had to have some explanation. Surely everything I believed wasn't a lie. Surely. Or maybe this was a good thing?

Also, just so you know, I'm not making up this experience, or that response. My friend did have a great time, but the following week after the awakening experience she was tormented in the night with severe anxiety, fear, panic attacks, and nightmares. As we share our experiences, both of us ended up coming back to the Lord and repenting for opening that door.

Chapter 21

The Pier

Frantically as I stood there on the pier I had driven to the morning after the Kundalini experience, I journaled. I looked up numbers to find significance in my experience. It's hard to describe that feeling But I knew something, everything was changing.

Standing on this same pier had been an altar to me so many times. I stood in this spot before I went off to rehab. I stood on this pier before I went back to the school of ministry. I stood on this pier when I needed an answer from God. I stood there when I chose to move to South Asia. I stood there when I considered whether I should marry my husband. I had gone there to consider divorce (which didn't happen, thankfully). And again, on this day, I stood there, searching like never before.

Dolphins jumped in the distance, and tears streamed down my face. Something was happening. How could I still claim to worship, serve, adore, and love Jesus, but also worship, serve, love, and even adore Ganesh, Lakshmi, Lord Shiva, and the sweet, cute Buddha? They were in no way the same. It was a weak claim and contrary to everything I *knew* to be true. And it was not fair to pretend I was following all routes that led to the truth, when I hadn't cracked open a Bible in months, if not a year. I was onto something, even though I didn't really want it to be true.

I turned to a faithful new friend in my search for answers. ChatGPT.

"My suicide attempt was on 11/24. What's significant about numbers 11 and 24?" I read the answers. Weak.

"Hey ChatGPT, what does the Bible say in scriptures with 11:24?"

> "1. MARK 11:24 "THEREFORE, I TELL YOU, WHATEVER YOU ASK IN PRAYER, BELIEVE THAT YOU HAVE RECEIVED IT, AND IT WILL BE YOURS." SIGNIFICANCE: THIS VERSE EMPHASIZES FAITH AND THE POWER OF PRAYER. IT IS OFTEN INTERPRETED AS A REMINDER TO TRUST IN GOD'S TIMING AND HAVE UNWAVERING FAITH IN YOUR DESIRES MANIFESTING."

Okay.... I read on, Hebrews 11:24, ok. I read on, Deuteronomy 11:24. Ok... Then it happened.

> "4. JOHN 11:24 "MARTHA SAID TO HIM, 'I KNOW THAT HE WILL RISE AGAIN IN THE RESURRECTION AT THE LAST DAY.'" SIGNIFICANCE: THIS VERSE SPEAKS TO HOPE AND FAITH IN THE PROMISE OF RESURRECTION. IT REFLECTS TRUST IN GOD'S PLAN AND THE ETERNAL LIFE OFFERED THROUGH CHRIST."

As soon as I read these words, I crumbled. On my own historic altar, The Holy Spirit spoke, breaking the silence from God I had brought upon myself from years of not listening anymore. I know it wasn't verbatim to the verse, but when searching for the reason for everything happening in life, on December 8th, early in the morning, I heard clearly the voice of the Lord call me back to Him.

"I have resurrected you, now act like it."

. . .

My soul ignited. That was it. That was my call.

I didn't need to rise to my highest self, I needed to come out of the grave. I wasn't needing light language, I needed the Light of the World. I wasn't looking for energy, I desperately needed the power of the Holy Spirit.

He was still the same, I was the one who had changed. His voice was still clear. It was still holy. He was still good. He was the One who protected me in the hospital and woke me up. He was the one who protected me when I called out the night before. The One who never left.

Overwhelmed by this encounter, I was shocked when my friends came to meet me. "Play it cool," I told myself. But I couldn't. Inside of my heart was years of unfinished business and thwarted plans with the Lord. I needed to be alone with the Lord and sort this out. I said my goodbyes after breakfast and hit the road.

I began to pray immediately, in tongues, because I didn't quite have the words. As I prayed my head began to clear. I would've prayed for hours but I had one pitstop to make along the way.

Immediately after my time at the pier, I called the same friend whom I had visited many years before on Memorial Day after the first suicide attempt over a decade ago. She was a trusted voice in my life, having been there for season after season. As I sat with her, told her everything—again. My story stunned and disappointed her, but I continued to tell her about my encounter the night before and earlier that morning. And I told her that somehow, I felt "sober-minded" for the first time in a long time. Though it had only been a couple of hours, she agreed and said she's not heard me talk so clearly before, which was crazy considering how

I was spiraling. Though hardly any time had passed, I told her confidently that I was back with the Lord, and that I needed a church. It was odd that that was the first thing I wanted after encountering Jesus again. She asked about my plan, and I told her one.

And that's when the whirlwind picked me up.

Chapter 22

The Whirlwind

I had no idea how beautiful God was writing a story for me.

Within a week of all this happening, I was intentional to get to safety. For me that meant seeing people who had gone through multiple seasons with me and visiting places where I had once encountered the Lord. So, I revisited the place in Alabama where I'd gone to ministry school. After I had attempted suicide I reached out to a friend at that church. To see her and other people who prayed for me in such a desperate time was surreal. They knew my pain, and they saw me broken. But being seen by people, hugging people, and knowing they genuinely loved me, it moved me. I wasn't alone. How incredibly healing for a fragile soul.

I was working my way throughout the southeast on a work trip, and it worked out that the next night after that, I could attend a revival service in Kentucky. On the five-hour drive there, I spent the entire time in prayer—sincerely repenting, renouncing the enemy, asking the spirit of God to help me and fill me again. I didn't know how it would all make sense, or how logistically in a fallen life everything could work together. But I knew now that I could not settle for anything less than serving the Lord and loving Him with all my heart, mind, soul, and strength.

I had gone to this Kentucky revival to see an old ministry school instructor and mentor from fourteen years before. I hadn't heard of or from him in so long, but I knew that he had always been so passionate about the Word of God having first place in our lives and about the person-hood of the Holy Spirit, among many other things. The beautiful providence of God is that he'd be there at the exact time I'd be driving through, and I don't know that I would've gone for any other reason. Since safety in the Lord was my goal, sitting under his preaching for my first service back in a traditional church felt okay, and even appropriate. I knew him enough to know he wouldn't waver from the Word.

When I got there, I was shaking before I even walked in the sanctuary. When I walked inside, I slipped into the back row as to hide, but in church they like to greet people. I was just planning to come, listen to the message, and I'd maybe say hi to Pastor Jason when I was leaving. I was so uncom-fortable when I was sitting there. The pastor of the church came to say hi. When he introduced himself to me, he asked my name. As soon as I told him he smiled and said,

> "Oh! You're the missionary Jason told me about. It's good
> to see you. There's a seat for you up front next to Jason."

I smiled my way through the small talk, pulling on every former experience of holding a façade as I could. I was crushed inside.

Apparently, Pastor Jason did remember me, though I hadn't expected him to or to even know I was coming. I'd just messaged his wife. But he remembered, and apparently, he still knew of me as a missionary. How embarrassing, and how disappointed he would be when he saw me and found out that was not the case. I didn't go up front, instead when the pastor walked away, I located my nearest exit and made my plan to leave before I saw him. As I was starting to fumble through my stuff, I heard him call me.

"Well well well, if it isn't Danica" and fondly recalled a story about where I was from.

My heart felt like it was going to beat out of my chest.
"Play it cool, Dan"
Pastor Jason had spoken many things into my life a decade before that and had still stood with me, so my respect for him was still great even after all those years. While catching up, he asked what I was doing now and without meaning to, I spilled over as much as I could of what had just happened in my life. Though he could have, he didn't really react to what I said, which is honestly surprising. He just shook my hand, said it was good to see me, and told me to sit in the front row next to him, I followed him, and the service started.

I was a nervous wreck, but I remember specifically that worship was so amazing that night. When they sang about Jesus being the Name above all names and His name being higher, I meant it with everything in me when I sang it along. Those songs carried much more weight than they ever had before, as I had never allowed myself to walk in idolatry before in any other season of life. As worship continued, it was overwhelming. Though I had just had a crazy week of coming back to the Lord, condemnation pressed me and the guilt and remembrance of all I'd done lingered in my mind. I was embarrassed to be on the front row and felt very out of place. I was uncomfortable, but somehow, I knew I had come to the right place at the right time.

But in my mind, I still had serious doubts about what to do next. My kids were still in India, my husband was not a Christian, my entire community was Hindu, and there was no church around that I knew to go to. I felt overwhelmed. *"Now what do I do? Can I even keep my life and still follow Jesus? Because I don't really want to... but I know He's the truth and I'll lay it all down, whatever it takes."* I was ready to walk away completely if it meant following Jesus. I was willing to pay the cost to follow Jesus, but the weight of that really hurt.

While he preached, Pastor Jason flowed through scripture after scripture beautifully. Though I'll be honest, I don't remember the exact message—I'm sure he forgives me for that. So much was happening within me. When he spoke the Word, every single word pierced through me. It also somehow felt like I was taking a shower and finally getting clean after rolling through the mud. A true pig pen redemptive experience.

If that wasn't enough, a word of knowledge was released from the platform that was exactly what I needed to hear concerning my questions about the future. Uncontrollably, I sobbed. That's when Pastor Jason leaned over and simply said,

"The Holy Ghost is trying to help you, Danica."

I swigged a drink of water, swallowed hard, preparing myself for what was about to happen, and said,

"I know."

It was that pre-altar call feeling all over again. But this time, less daunting—this time I knew I was safe.

He asked a prophet friend of his to come over to pray over me. Since he acknowledged him as a prophet, I got ready for my word. I braced myself.

"The Lord wants me to tell you that He's not mad at you for what has happened."

Not what I was expecting. Then he hugged me. I couldn't even show my face—I was so overwhelmed. No one, in seven years, had intentionally hugged me. Seven years. I had always felt isolated, unseen, and alone. I knew it was the Lord in that moment.

Shortly after that, another person praying for me said the Lord would reveal to me how He felt about me in a single word and prayed for me to hear it. Like a mini little sozo session in a single prayer, if you know what that is. I heard nothing, so she prayed again, and I didn't really expect much. But I kid you not, it's as serious to me now, writing this, as it was at that moment.

I didn't "hear" anything. My mind was still far too full to catch a still, small voice. But what I *felt* at that moment was more than I could explain. For the first time in over a decade, I felt surrounded. I felt heard. I felt seen. I felt understood. I felt held.

I felt loved.

I wasn't alone anymore, and that was true.

That was my moment to ask the Lord, *"If you will, make me clean."* And just as He was with the leper in the Gospels, He was also moved with compassion *for me.*

He touched *me*.

The dirty, unclean, mess of a failed missionary—stuck in one sin after another and had done terrible things. I had missed the mark over and over, but He still wanted to make me clean. He was willing.

As I felt His presence, my body could no longer take it, and I collapsed on the floor and wept. I cried and cried as I encountered the Lord in such a deeply personal way. It was clear to me: I was home. This was right.

And the most beautiful journey began. Finally, I was home, in Him.

The whirlwind continued while the Lord healed my heart with undeserved connection. The day after I went to the Western Kentucky Revival, I drove up to Louisville and took a flight down to Miami, where I was able to meet yet another mentor from ministry school. Before I shared my story, I joked,

> "Please don't look at me with 'Jesus eyes' while I tell you this. I can't take it right now."

He laughed—and if you know him, you know I meant it. This Pastor was the Grace & Truth guy. Genuine through and through and having coffee with someone I so deeply respected was surreal.

He didn't hold back his tears when I told him my story, and he spoke truth, prophesied over me, declaring a change of appetite in my desires, and he even gave me practical advice. I was so humbled. He quoted something that marked me deeply: "God writes straight on crooked lines." And prayed for me sincerely.

Those kinds of connections, reconnections, new meetings, and services continued to happen. I had personal meetings with some of my heroes in the faith.

But something more beautiful than that happened. I was so deeply affected by the work the Lord had done in my life, just like Pastor Micah had prophesied over me, my appetite completely changed. And not overtime, but immediately. I was hungry and thirsty for righteousness. I couldn't sleep; I could hardly eat. So, I just dove into the Bible, reading as much as I could. I finished the New Testament in just a few days. The words washed over me, and I realized—Jesus meant it when He said He would make me clean.

Chapter 23

The Lie

I can't continue any longer without telling you how serious I am about this one fact. *I didn't mean to be deceived.* No one ever does.

I was the girl who grew up in church and went to ministry school. The girl who, against all odds, went on and became a full-time missionary—and not even in an "easy" place. I wasn't trying to lose my way. I was searching for healing. For peace. For freedom.

When my heart felt unstable, and I let go of that hope I once had as an anchor, and I let myself wander out to find something else to hold on to. At first what I had found seemed beautiful. It was soft. It seemed like it finally made sense. And it felt good, offering peace. To compromise on little things that didn't seem to matter. To drink here and there if I was overwhelmed. To meditate, manifest, and align, do a little yoga for "my health". To eventually be the big bad boss girl I knew I could and should be. It offered me a sense of peace, and it seemed to work at first.

The anxiety dulled. The rituals gave me structure. The affirmations made me feel strong.

Mrs. I-N-D-E-P-E-N-D-E-N-T had control, a firm grip and grasp on life. I was motivated, empowered, strong. I had good lip service, and my responses and statuses were insightful, so I felt like I was in a good place. It even made sense if you really thought about some of the things I said, I thought. Wise in my own eyes.

It felt spiritual. It felt empowering. It was logical and semi-scientific. But it wasn't Jesus. Hope was no longer my anchor, but trust in my own abilities held me. I felt good in who I was becoming. And that's the thing about deception: it doesn't feel wrong when you're in it. It feels right. Even holy. I felt like it was my new purpose in life to lead people away from the religious church and into a more universalist lifestyle even. It was deconstruction and breaking down the "falsities" I had grown up believing. It was opening my mind, broadening my views. It felt good, because I had found something. And sadly, I didn't even realize that little by little the grip the enemy had on my life was swallowing me whole.

Because the enemy doesn't usually show up with horns and a sign that says, "I am destruction." Rather,

"For even Satan disguises himself as an angel of light." (2 Corinthians 11:14 ESV)

This disguise allows us to feel like we are in absolute control, but we will find that we struggle to breathe as his grip gets tighter. As the cares of this world laid heavier on me, instead of casting them on Jesus, I took control and held on tighter to the cares that weighed me down.

I didn't leave the truth and run straight into darkness, eager to destroy everything I had spent years building with the Holy Spirit. I wasn't eager to fall away, but I had settled for something that looked close enough to what I really wanted, and even perhaps it seemed more alluring. See, the counterfeit life gave me all I wanted with no need for consecration.

There were no glaring red flags, but instead just subtle redirections. There were small shifts in my language and beliefs, tiny compromises here and there until I was engulfed.

Suddenly, I wasn't praying to a Savior—I was talking to "the universe." I grew cold to the saving power of the blood, and grew bored of the idea of traditional Christianity, feeling like it was outdated and incomplete. I wasn't surrendering to God, I was manifesting my desires and putting myself first. It felt justified, since I had already truly lived a life of sacrifice. I was no longer actively repenting, but I was trying to raise my vibration, become my higher self. In doing so, I found just how wrong everyone around me seemed to be.

But at the end of the day, I was still empty. Deep down, I was still tormented, just as alone. Just as desperate and still tired. Because the counterfeit can mimic peace, but hear me friend it cannot deliver you.

I was deceived, and confused. And I felt smart, but I didn't even know what I believed anymore. Even up until the day of the Kundalini retreat, I hadn't admitted to myself that I was following New Age teachings. I wouldn't have outwardly labeled myself a universalist. I thought I was just "open," "curious," "spiritual," and even "deconstructed."

I had made quiet agreements with ideas I never tested against God's Word. And that's how deception often works. It doesn't always come through intentional rebellion. Sometimes it comes through redefinition. You start thinking:

"I believe in Jesus, but..." "I don't think God would ever..." "My truth is just..." "All paths probably lead to the same source..."

And without realizing it, you mold Jesus into your own image, and you weaken His power by creating an idol with the same name, but who looks nothing like Him. A false god *named* Jesus, but stripped of His Holiness and detached from His cross. Sad. He becomes reduced to another spiritual option that has no real power. Hear me beloved, Jesus isn't an option. He is Lord.

If you could have zoomed out and looked at my life from above, you would have seen what I couldn't. You would have seen the drift. The drinking, the partying, the slow disconnect from my family. The acceptance and tolerance of things that once would have broken my heart. The lost consecration.

I didn't see it, because I wasn't measuring my life against the Word of God. I wasn't using the Bible as a mirror or letting the Holy Spirit lead me. Had I done so, I would have seen how far off course I was and corrected myself with repentance in the fear of the Lord. Instead, I was measuring my life by how I *felt*. And emotions, untethered from truth, are terrible guides, they were never meant to lead.

Even after my experience with the Lord after that kundalini retreat, for two weeks I was still living in ways that didn't align with Him, though I did want something more. I just didn't grasp the depth of the deception or the depravity of my sin and how far away I had walked. It's a process.

And when I walked into that revival and the Word of

God began to wash over me, I finally understood again.nBe-
cause it's the Word that brings light.

> *"The entrance of Your Word gives light; it gives*
> *understanding to the simple."* (Psalm 1 1 9:1 3 0)

As the Word was preached, something began to break
open in me. Light flooded where darkness had hidden, and
the truth of God's word exposed the lies that I had made
peace with and I realized just how far I had wandered.

When the real Jesus, (not the new age deconstructed
idol I had created) came crashing into my darkness, I experienced the power of the Resurrected King. The Lion of
Judah. And he didn't offer me a new affirmation and recom-
mend a specific crystal, He once again revealed Himself to
me, and offered me Himself. Nail-scarred. Risen. Uncom-
promising. Merciful. Just. Loving. Steadfast. and
Unwavering.

He said, "Come home," and He let me come to Him
just as I was, but He would not leave me there. It didn't take
much time before he showed me that the very sin I had
clung to for comfort was the sin He had been crucified for.
He reminded me that real comfort doesn't come from
coping and getting by—it comes from the cross.

> *"For the joy set before Him, He endured the cross, despising*
> *the shame, and is seated at the right hand of the throne of*
> *God."* (Hebrews 1 2:2)

The joy set before Him, was for me. What kind of love
is that? I had believed a series of lies that brought my life
into destruction. I thought that I didn't need saving—only a
higher level of awakening. I thought that healing my inner

child, aligning my energy, working with a light healer and speaking affirmations would make me whole.

But I didn't need enlightenment, I needed *the Light*. I didn't need another ritual, I needed repentance, I needed to change.

There's a common misconception or lie of the enemy that because "Jesus loves me just the way I am" that He would not expect change from me or call me higher, but rather He would be tolerant to my ways and habits, even if they were sin. But that misconception in its half-truth, misleading jargon is this:

Yes, Jesus meets you exactly where you are. He's not afraid to touch the leper, but when you meet the real Jesus —He never leaves you there. He doesn't just touch the leper, He cleanses him. But it's worth noticing that the leper still approached Jesus.

When we give Him room, He touches the parts we hide, and He confronts the things we excuse. He calls us higher, but He gives the grace to come. And it's one thing to feel His love, but another thing completely to surrender your life to it.

Jesus offends the religious spirit. He offends the compromised soul.

He offends the mind that says, 'Surely God didn't mean that.' But He never apologizes for His standard. He simply says:

"Come."

And you'll either follow— or you'll reshape Him into something more palatable.But reshaping Him isn't faith, it's idolatry, and it is death.

And I promise you this: The real Jesus, as He is—the

same yesterday, today, and forever, is worth everything it costs to follow Him.

Chapter 24

The Cleansing

After confronting the deception that had subtly taken hold of my life, I knew there was only one way forward: I had to be utterly ruthless with anything that stood between me and God.

I began by cleansing my home. Every literal idol, every artifact that didn't honor God was thrown out. The display of alcohol that had once been a centerpiece in my family room was dismantled. Every hidden foothold was exposed and removed; I didn't have time to play games.

I anointed every room with oil, praying over my household and reclaiming it for the Lord. I disposed of every substance, every object, every habit that wasn't aligned with His will.

It was a radical, practical step—and a declaration that I would no longer allow any territory in my life for the enemy to occupy. I wouldn't live a life of tolerance to permissible things that still stood between me and my Savior. I knew that to walk in radical obedience to Him, and to live utterly dependent upon Him, that I could have no crutch other than His grace.

This path of radical obedience wasn't just a season or a phase. It was a transformative commitment, and I still walk in it today. I know what it was like to "cut corners" or allow things that weren't sin but also weren't good. No thanks, I'll not go back. Radical obedience wasn't a moment of being ruthless, it became a lifestyle.

A lifestyle of consecration says, *"What can I do to be more like You? How can I walk in holiness and be pleasing to the Lord in word and deed?"*

As I took these steps, the opposition wasn't just a subtle misunderstanding. People ridiculed me, and even other Christians may have looked at me as if I was doing "the most." Those who didn't know Jesus made fun of me, and of the Word. They spoke and acted in ways meant to hurt because they didn't understand why I was changing—or why I couldn't go back to my old ways.

But I vowed to live a life that removes excuses for others. Just as Noah was found righteous in the eyes of the Lord, and moved in faith when it seemed irrational, excessive, and even silly to all those around him—I decided that if it didn't lead me closer to Jesus, it wasn't for me.

Now understand, I was still living within a culture where actual idol worship and worldly practices were not just normal—they were celebrated. It wasn't just your traditional western idolatry of sports and television—people in my life worship literal demons in order to feel blessed. And as a wife to someone who didn't yet share my faith, the tension was real.

It would have been easy to compromise—to hold onto my old ways to avoid looking "extreme" or "holier than thou." I could've done things that *weren't bad* but kept the peace, but I simply couldn't.

I knew the cost, and I drew a line in the sand, and I

continue to draw those lines daily. Because it's worth it to me to take authority over my life and stand for the truth. It's worth it even if it feels like I stand alone, which I don't. All of heaven backs me, which is so much sweeter than a handful of people who don't care about eternity.

"Do not be conformed to this world, but be transformed by the renewing of your mind." (Romans 12:2, ESV)

This transformation wasn't about outward behavior modification. It was about daily renewing my mind and choosing to believe God's Word over my emotions. It was choosing to let Scripture, not culture, define me.

Practically, it looked like cutting off distractions. Replacing hours of television and social media with prayer, worship, and Scripture. It meant setting a standard for what I would allow in my life and home. It looked like guarding what I allowed into my home and in my heart. It meant deleting contacts, Spotify playlists, not watching certain shows or reading certain books anymore. It meant taking every thought captive and making it obedient to Christ. It wasn't about being legalistic, because I had done that. This was about being holy for Him. It was my response to a changed life.

And slowly, surely, my appetites changed. The things that once entertained me now repulsed me and the conversations I used to crave now grieved me. The old desires faded as new desires took root. I wasn't missing out; I wasn't better than anyone else. But I was coming alive, and I was pressing into my Savior.

The more I pressed into God, the more He drew near to me. The more I laid things down, the more He filled me with Himself. The more I chose to renew my mind, the more He transformed my life. Depression lost its grip. Suicidal thoughts were silenced. Anxiety ceased. Physical repercussions from my life of sin vanished. A ruthless life was not a burden. It was freedom, and it opened the door for real joy.

It was the beginning of a new way of living—ruthless to anything that pulled me away, and reckless in love for the One who had called me home. But even as my outward life shifted, something even more important was happening inside me. I wasn't just throwing out idols, I was discovering who I really was.

During this season, I devoured books that pointed me back to the Word of God and teachings that agreed with and highlighted scripture. I clung to the Scriptures that declared I was the righteousness of God in Christ (2 Corinthians 5:21). I wasn't trying to earn my place anymore. I realized the veil had been torn (Matthew 27:51), and I could come boldly before the throne of grace (Hebrews 4:16).

I wasn't distant from God; I was accepted. I wasn't disqualified; I was made new. The Word became my anchor. It wasn't about striving or performing, it was about standing in what Jesus had already accomplished. It was about finally believing Him, and it was foundation for me.

"For I am confident of this very thing, that He who began a good work in you will perfect it until the day of Christ Jesus."
(Philippians 1:6)

Chapter 25

The Return

I thank God every day that He rescued me. To have a second, third, fourth chance at life is beautiful and I am so undeserving of how good He has been to me. But I want you to know from my story that the Lord doesn't stop at the rescue. He doesn't deliver us and leave us there. He also restores, He helps us rebuild. And in His faithfulness, He not only restores what was stolen, but even what I squandered away. He could have just saved my life and let me go on about my business until it was time to go to heaven. But when God restores, He brings it back redeemed and marked by His hand. He is extravagant in every way, and His plan is bigger than just us.

My trip back to India had been planned long before my return home encounter with the Lord. The plan had always been to reunite my family, bringing my children and in-laws home to the United States. But during my darkest moments, especially amidst suicidal thoughts and sitting in an empty home, it was easy to forget that. The darkness clouded my vision, making it impossible to see beyond the pain. Yet, even when I couldn't see a future, God remained faithful to His promises.

As the plane touched down, there was a stillness in my spirit I hadn't known before. It reminded me of that first trip back in 2016, but there was a greater confidence and depth to my excitement. I didn't feel the fear or anxiety that once gripped me when I thought of India. I didn't even feel the grief of all that I had left behind. I felt absolute peace and assurance—not from circumstances, but from Him.

This wasn't a return in defeat, or another trip that reminded me of all I had lost and squandered away with my decisions, it was a return under His covering and felt redemptive through and through.

Seeing my daughter and son again was indescribable. Like all the chaos in the world was cleared and everything was right and according to His plan again. The enemy had tried to separate us, but God had made a way. When I was holding them, I was reminded that nothing can separate us from the love of Christ—not even our worst moments.

I spent those early days soaking them in, praying over them, and speaking the name of Jesus into their lives. But it wasn't just about my family. God was stirring something deeper.

As I walked through the streets and sat with people in their homes, I felt His heart beating for the Indian people again, louder than ever before. This time, it wasn't through the lens of pain but through the lens of hope.

He hadn't just restored my family; He was reigniting the call He had placed on my life. I felt purpose pulsing through me and stirring me to hold on amid hardship as the trip back wasn't easy. And it was chaotic, emotional, and stretching in ways I hadn't anticipated.

The invitations to drift didn't disappear because I had

changed; if anything, they became louder as people didn't understand the new boundaries I walked in. Temptations arose, but the Bible says to resist the devil, and he will flee from you. So, I resisted, and God had made me steadfast. I wasn't bending anymore.

During that trip, something else also happened—something painful. I miscarried for the second time while trying for our third baby. It was a loss that hurt deeply and tested my heart in unexpected ways. After recovering from a season of significant loss and what felt unfair over an over it was an "icing on the cake" type moment in the negative sense. My unsaved husband at the time, seeing my faith growing stronger, also struggled to understand. *"If God is who He says He is, why would this happen?"* It wasn't an easy question or season. In my carnal mind, it would've made sense for God to bless me and flourish me to draw my husband to Him.

But for the first time, I saw clearly that this loss was not authored by God. God is not the thief, He is the Giver of Life. The enemy is the one who comes to steal, kill, and destroy. I made the decision not to accuse God of what the enemy had done. I aligned my thinking with the truth: God is good, period.

Instead of letting bitterness take root, that pain became fuel—a fire to stand firmer, a reminder to take authority over the enemy's plans and refuse to surrender ground. I wasn't backing down—not now, not ever.

Even during grief, God was present. He opened doors for me to share Jesus with my husband, his family, and others in the community who had never truly heard the Gospel. With a greater level of influence into the Indian community than I ever had before, though they didn't agree —they listened.

It wasn't perfect or eloquent, but it was honest, and sometimes, that's all God needs to plant a seed. Amidst the challenges, I experienced an overwhelming sense of joy. Not a fleeting happiness, but a deep-seated joy that the Bible describes as a fruit of the Spirit (Galatians 5:22).

This joy wasn't dependent on my circumstances but was rooted in my relationship with God. It was a testament to His presence in my life, even during trials.

As I embraced this joy, I found strength and hope, knowing that God's promises are true and His love unwavering. This trip wasn't just a mission to restore my family; it was the beginning of a bigger story.

It was a new season; one marked by both warfare and promise. God used that trip to reignite dreams I thought were dead, to remind me that the Indian people are still on His heart, and that His plans are never canceled.

Returning to India didn't mark the end of a battle; it marked the beginning of a new one. But this time, I wasn't fighting for survival; I was standing in victory. Not because I was strong, but because He is.

And no matter what lay ahead, I knew this much was settled: Jesus had already overcome.

Chapter 26

The Restoration

"God sets the lonely in families." (Psalm 68:6)

This brings us to what you could call the current chapter in my life, the one where the Lord continues to heal and restore. He's healed my sense of belonging—something I had so desperately desired but had buried deep under disappointment, mistrust, and loneliness.

After the suicide attempt that could have ended everything, God didn't just save my life. Through His faithfulness, He also began restoring everything I thought was too broken to hope for—including family, community, and my place in His Body, the church.

It was hard to even admit how much I needed people. I had spent years guarding myself, believing I was safer alone, believing the lie that isolation was strength and that to get somewhere quicker you needed to go alone. The feeling of being misunderstood pushed me further into loneliness.

But in the earliest days after my rescue, something beautiful began to happen. Multiple people, without knowing the full depth of my private wrestle, began speaking the same words to me repeatedly:

"You are not alone."

But it wasn't just a comforting Christianized kind of word, it was confirmation to me, and they said those words as if they truly meant them. It was so lovingly expressed and deeply felt, that I felt like family to them.

God was answering the silent cries I had pushed down for years. He was telling me:

"I haven't only rescued you—I've placed you among My people."

Not long after, He did something even more remarkable. He reconnected me and connected me with people from all over the body of Christ. New friends and leaders, with friends who were still serving the Lord but I hadn't spoken to in years, and voices from earlier seasons of my life. It was crazy. Relationships that had seemed long dormant suddenly stirred back to life. Healing those places in my heart and dismantling the lie that I was forgotten and unloved.

But even though God was moving, I knew I had a responsibility too. I didn't want to wander anymore. I wasn't called to be a lone wolf, out here to do life with just me and Jesus.

I was called to be part of a flock. I knew I needed to go back to the church. To the very place that I once had felt broke me. I didn't trust myself enough to pick a church based on my preferences, because I could've searched for years for that. I wanted to be led by the Spirit.

So, I asked some of the leaders if they knew of a church in my city. They told me about a church where they knew the Word was being taught and the Spirit of God was moving.

Contrary to how I had relearned to live life, in a consumer mindset that tries it out first and then commits after, I felt the Lord call me to be decisive. Before I ever set foot through the door, I decided in prayer, and I told the Lord:

> "If the Word is truly taught, if Your Spirit is at liberty to move, if this is a place where I can grow, and where the church can grow, then this will be my home."

It wouldn't matter if the style was different from what I was used to. And it was. It wouldn't matter if everything felt comfortable right away. And it was not. I made up my mind that I would plant myself where God's presence and God's Word were honored. Belonging wasn't about finding the *perfect* fit. It was about obeying the perfect Shepherd.

And once I made that decision, peace settled over me. I wasn't looking anymore. I wasn't wandering anymore. I was home. Even though I didn't know everyone yet, there was a corporate anointing—a tangible atmosphere of belonging and presence.

I could feel it every time I walked through the doors: I was where I was supposed to be. The loneliness that once seemed permanent was beginning to break. And it wasn't emotional hype—it was the Word and the Spirit of at work.

I began to realize that restoration wasn't just personal—it was corporate.

I wasn't just reconciled to God. I was being restored to His family.

"Consequently, you are no longer strangers and foreigners,

but fellow citizens with the saints and members of the
household of God, having been built on the foundation of the
apostles and prophets, Christ Jesus Himself being the
cornerstone." (Ephesians 2:19–20)

I wasn't surviving on the outskirts anymore; I was being built into the household of God. And He wasn't just healing my wounds. He was securing my place.

And then came a deeper revelation. One day, as I was reading through Ephesians 1 and 2, familiar passages suddenly came alive. Paul spoke about the resurrection of Jesus—how Christ was raised from the dead and seated in heavenly places at the right hand of the Father. And then he said something astonishing:

"God raised us up with Christ and seated us with Him in the
heavenly realms in Christ Jesus." (Ephesians 2:6)

We weren't just forgiven. We were raised with Him. As I sat there reading, a memory stirred—one I hadn't thought of in years. I remembered ministry school and I remembered an instructor teaching us about the authority believers have because of our union with the risen Christ.

How when Jesus was raised, the Body was raised with Him. How authority flows not individually, but through the connection of the Body to the Head.

And it clicked.

I wasn't just meant to believe in Jesus personally. I was meant to live connected to Him corporately, as part of His Body. And as part of His mission, in Ephesians it says according to HIS calling. Not just mine.

I realized that my years of isolation—my "just me and

Jesus" mindset—hadn't been protecting my faith. It had been crippling it.

If I am part of the Body and Jesus is the Head, then refusing to stay planted and connected wasn't just hurting me—it was causing dysfunction in the Body itself. A disconnected body part can't fulfill its purpose, and it cannot survive. It becomes a point of weakness, not strength.

My isolation wasn't a badge of strength. It was an open wound, a desperate cry for help. And even more painfully, I realized I wasn't just hurting myself. I was limiting what Christ wanted to reveal through me.

"If the whole body were an eye, where would the sense of hearing be? If the whole body were an ear, where would the sense of smell be? But now God has arranged the parts, each one of them in the body, just as He desired." (1 Corinthians 12:17–18)

Every member matters. Every function matters. I mattered, and so did they. As that truth settled deeper into my spirit, another realization followed: I didn't want to be the one to handicap the power of Christ's resurrection by refusing to be part of, and love, His Church. Jesus didn't just rise to save isolated individuals.

He rose to raise a Body, a living Church full of many members, functioning together under His Headship. Refusing connection wasn't just a personal loss. It resisted His design. It was restricting His power throughout my life.

If I loved Him, I would love what He loved. If I honored His resurrection, I would honor His Body. No more withholding. No more half-in faith.

I was all His and that meant I was theirs too. Restoration wasn't just emotional. It was strategic. God wasn't just healing my loneliness. He was restoring me to authority—authority that flows only through connection.

"And He put all things under His feet and gave Him as head over all things to the Church, which is His Body, the fullness of Him who fills all in all." (Ephesians 1:22–23)

The Body is His fullness on the earth. The Body is how His life, power, and presence move. When I disconnected, I lived weakened. When I reconnected, His life began to flow through me again and stronger, freer, and fuller than ever before.

And it wasn't because of perfect people; it was because of a perfect Savior who chose to move through imperfect vessels.

This restoration is still unfolding; it's my current address as I watch in amazement as deep wounds heal week by week. Friendships continue to grow, ministry opportunities are starting to bud. And I am still at the beginning of this journey as I write, but it's a powerful thing the Lord has already done in my life.

I am planted and positioned. I am part of the living, breathing Body of Christ. And belonging to Him and belonging to His people has healed places in me I didn't even realize were bleeding.

I am no longer a wandering believer trying to survive on my own. I am a daughter rooted in my Father's house. A flourishing member of Christ's living Body, and a vessel ready to carry His love into the world.

And that love rooted me, healed me, and restored my authority. And little did I know that when I just chose my church with a steadfast heart, that the love of Jesus and the power of His might was about to crash into my life in a way

I had never known. The love and power of God wasn't just something I would hear about. It was about to become my reality.

And it has been so, so good.

> *"Those who are planted in the house of the LORD*
> *Shall flourish in the courts of our God.*
> *They shall still bear fruit in old age;*
> *They shall be fresh and flourishing,*
> *To declare that the LORD is upright;*
> *He is my rock, and there is no unrighteousness in Him."*
> *Psalm 92:13-15*

Chapter 27

The End of Myself

As you've read in my story, I had a beautiful life with the Lord, my Father. I knew Him. I had seen His power, known His voice, and walked with Him in ways many never have done. But I walked away. Not in one moment, but in hundreds of small ones.

I left because of unresolved pain, comparison, disappointment, disillusionment and lies, and the slow erosion of consecration until I no longer remembered what holiness felt like. I thought I was still close, still in reach, but I had wandered far. I was convinced there was more for me beyond Him. That I could carry the weight of my calling on my own shoulders. That maybe freedom looked like something else.

I sought my own ways of living, my own truths. I squandered everything the Father had given me—ending up in the mess of a muddy, smelly life. I took everything He gave me and wasted it. I chased empty promises, and I drank from broken cisterns. I lived in contradiction, trying to hold onto a little bit of God while holding hands with the world.

Until eventually, all that was left was mud. And I didn't even feel worthy to return.

It's the story Jesus told in Luke 15.

"Then He said: 'A certain man had two sons. And the younger of them said to his father, "Father, give me the portion of goods that falls to me." So he divided to them his livelihood. And not many days after, the younger son gathered all together, journeyed to a far country, and there wasted his possessions with prodigal living. But when he had spent all, there arose a severe famine in that land, and he began to be in want. Then he went and joined himself to a citizen of that country, and he sent him into his fields to feed swine. And he would gladly have filled his stomach with the pods that the swine ate, and no one gave him anything.'" (Luke 15:11–16 NKJV)

The younger son had gone as far as he could go. That distance was thrilling when he had control, when he had resources. But now? Now, it was a prison.

I know that feeling. I had been feasting, then suddenly I woke up one day and I was famished. Surrounded by things I thought I wanted, but I was empty and alone. My once-costly robe was now tattered, heavy with mud, and stripped of its meaning.

Just as the prodigal longed to fill his stomach with the pigs' food, I too know what it's like to settle for less than the Father's table. My own "mud" was a life of compromise and sin, a heart so far from God that even His name on my lips felt counterfeit.

One day, in the story, the son "came to himself." I did too. I couldn't do it anymore. What I thought would give me freedom had kept me bound. I had failed too much and hurt too many people. I brought shame to the very body I once loved and served. But somewhere in the wreckage of my rebellion, I knew I had to go home. I knew I was on foreign territory I did not belong in.

On His way home, the prodigal rehearsed his speech, head low and heart pounding. He knew what waited for him was ceremonial shame. The kaddish. He could already hear the clay pots shattered at his feet to declare he was cut off forever. He could feel the spit of the elders. And knew already that he'd be banished by his own community.

It was heartbreaking, and I felt that too. Unsure of how anyone could trust me again, the dread of what my return might look like caused fear. But here's the beauty of the story—the prodigal's and mine.

"And he arose and came to his father. But when he was still a great way off, his father saw him and had compassion and ran and fell on his neck and kissed him." (Luke 15:20 NKJV)

The Father ran. Before the elders could reach him, before the pots could be broken, before the accusations could be shouted—He ran. I imagine robes flying, dust rising, face set on one thing: getting to His son first.

That's what He did for me. He came running.

It should've been the end. My heart had stopped. My body, lifeless on the table in that cold sterile room had given out. I had flatlined and it was finished. The beeping slowed and went silent. My soul lingered, searching, hoping, and wishing I wouldn't have done what I had just done. And my spirit was caught in the light of eternity. I knew what I deserved. I *wanted* to be held, but I deserved to be cast out. I needed mercy. I needed the Father.

He didn't wait. He didn't shame. He didn't list my failures. He shielded me from the stones of others, and He silenced the accusers and wrapped me in righteousness.

I didn't really deserve much. I was once an embarrassment. But instead of rejection, I was met with a robe, a ring, and a feast. The Father called me clean. He restored what I thought was lost forever. He sat me at tables I wasn't qualified to sit at. He grafted me back into His people, His church, His family.

That's what the love of the Father looks like. Not a passive invitation, but an all-out pursuit. He doesn't just let us return, He Himself makes sure we get there, and He leaves the 99 for the 1. And when we get home to Him, He throws a celebration.

That's my story. At the end of myself, I met the beginning of grace. This isn't a fairytale or a feel-good story. My friend, this is real life, and this is the Gospel. I should be dead. I should be forgotten. By now, the flowers on my grave would have faded. The grief of others would have long slowed down. Instead of six feet deep, I'm here. I'm alive and I'm not just breathing, but I'm burning. Resurrected. Redeemed. Recommissioned. I'm enjoying the party the Father has thrown for me, in His presence.

I came to the end of myself. And there, I found Jesus.

"I have been crucified with Christ. It is no longer I who live, but Christ who lives in me. And the life I now live in the flesh I live by faith in the Son of God, who loved me and gave himself for me." (Galatians 2:20 ESV)

Chapter 28

The Invitation

I know that you've read through my story now, and I appreciate you taking that little journey. But you should know, this story was never about me. I mean, yes—it's my life. But I'm part of a much bigger and beautiful story. One so extravagant that if I dwell on it too long, I'll just weep.

This story is about the love of a God who still rescues. The Jesus that came in grace and truth. The one who calls us to Him, but then in turn gives us the grace and ability we need to answer that call.

It's about the relentless mercy of a Savior who still calls prodigals' home. Who knows our downfalls but remembers His sacrifice. It's about a man, fully God, but who came as a man, who understands the cares of this world but still asks us to cast them on Him.

It's about Jesus, what He has done in my life, and what He wants to do in your life, too. I see now that each step, no matter how painful or imperfect, was carried by God's grace. It wasn't my strength, but His mercy, that brought me through. I am here today, not because I was perfect, which I know you can see in the chapters before, but because He was *faithful*.

He's so good. His mercy so rich to save us, ever enduring and forever patient. His grace, so powerful to pull us into purpose and help us walk worthy of His calling. And His blood that flowed freely. His sacrifice of His own life, becoming the Lamb of God, He took away the sins of the world.

He is good. He is kind. His mercies endure. He restores. He guides and leads. He has given us authority and leads us with His voice. His love, unlike anything any of us have ever experienced, is enough to thread through each of our stories and draw us to Him, so that we can have a life that resounds over and over in eternity.

If you feel that stirring inside, that pull to know Him more, or even at all, don't ignore it. That's not emotion and it didn't come from reading a story about a girl that couldn't get her act together. That's the Spirit of God, reaching for you.

My dear friend, you don't have to be perfect. You don't have to clean yourself up. You don't have to have all the answers. In a world where it's so important to search for the truth and create your own version of truth if you can't find it; I'm telling you, I have the answer for what you're seeking.

You just have to come home. Don't worry about what waits for you when you get there, I promise it's good! Open your heart to Him, and believe in Him. The same Jesus who rescued me stands ready to rescue you. The same power of the Holy Spirit that was with me at youth camp, with me in South Asia on the mission field, with me in rehab when I found His love all over again—is the same power that put breath back in my lungs when I laid lifeless on a cold emergency room table.

When I couldn't carry on anymore, He lifted me up. His power and His love and the integrity of who He is, is not just God the Creator, or God the Restorer, or God the Empowering One. Though He is all of that. His name and the character behind His name is going throughout the earth, drawing us to Him because He has already paid the price for our redemption. You're already written into His beautiful story, even if your chapter feels a little wonky right now.

The same love that pursued me is pursuing you. The same blood that washed me clean is enough for you. It doesn't matter where you find yourself now. You may be tired, worn out, broke, strung out, or just pushing through life trying to be good but feel like you still somehow miss the mark.

Or you may be done with religion, hurt by the church or those that were supposed to represent Christ but didn't do it well. You could be doing everything you can to disprove the Bible, or you may have spent this whole book annoyed because you don't even believe in a God—or worse, you see yourself as god. But I'm telling you, it's worth it to draw near. It doesn't have to be a long, drawn-out thing, it just must be real.

The Bible says,

"Everyone who calls on the name of the Lord will be saved."
(Romans 10:13)

I called out *"Holy Spirit, Protect me!"*
If you want to surrender your life to Jesus, it's as simple as a sincere prayer. And the Bible walks us through a simple 'formula' in Romans 10:8-10,

"But what does it say? "The word is near you, in your mouth and in your heart" (that is, the word of faith which we preach): that if you confess with your mouth the Lord Jesus and believe in your heart that God has raised Him from the dead, you will be saved. For with the heart, one believes unto righteousness, and with the mouth confession is made unto salvation."

It's simple, confess with your mouth (say it out loud, because your words have power) that Jesus is Lord and believe in your heart that He was raised from the dead (have faith that He is who He says He is), then you'll be saved.

Here's a little prayer if you want me to pray with you, I'd be honored to:

"Jesus, I believe You are the Son of God. I believe You died for my sins and rose again. I ask You to forgive me, to cleanse me, and to make me new. I surrender my life to You. Be my Savior. Be my Lord. Fill me with Your Spirit. Lead me into the life You have for me. I want to know You, to follow You, and to live for You — from this day forward. In Jesus' name, Amen."

If you prayed that prayer—then my friend, welcome home. Welcome into the family of God, what a glorious day this is for you! You're in the place where you belong. No longer alone, searching.

But this is just the beginning. Following Jesus isn't about a one-time decision — it's about a new life. It's about walking with Him daily, growing deeper in His love, and becoming who you were created to be.

Here are some practical next steps I encourage you to take, and when I say it's important—TRUST me, you want to do this.

Find a Bible-believing church. The church, though I claim it broke me, is the most beautiful gift Jesus gave to us aside from His own spirit and Himself. You need a church that will love you, believe with you, pray with you, and grow with you. And you need a pastor who will listen to the leading of the Holy Spirit and preach the whole truth of God's word.

Get a Bible and start reading it. *"Forever Oh Lord, Your Word is settled in Heaven"* (Psalm 119:89) The Word of God is life to us, and it is firmly fixed within eternity. His Word doesn't change, and there is so much power in it. When Jesus Himself was tempted in the wilderness, He fought the enemy with the Word. The Word is a sword, your greatest defense against the deception of the enemy. It's compared to be like a fire that consumes the things that are of no substance. And it is like a hammer that breaks the rock (even the stony, hardened places in our hearts) into pieces. We need it, period.

Pray daily. The Bible says my sheep know my voice and they follow me. We don't pray to fulfill a religious duty, but rather we spend time with the Lord to learn His nature, His voice, and His heart so that we can follow Him into the abundant life He promises us. Communion with Him, partnership in prayer, and time in His presence grows us stronger. My pastor calls it the pickling effect. Like a cucumber in vinegar, the more time in His presence, the more you'll never be able to go back to your old state.

Get baptized. And read Romans 6 before you do.

Baptism is a beautiful outward expression of the work Jesus has done on the inside of you. It's a symbol of dying to yourself and being resurrected with Him and let's all who see that you belong to the Lord. It's beautiful.

And my last piece of advice to all, whether you are more mature in your faith than I am, or you just prayed that prayer with me two minutes ago. **Stay hungry** — there's always more. We can go as far into the presence of God as we can handle, but do know, the further you're willing to go, the more costly it is to your flesh, but how gloriously so.

And know this, my friend, your story is far from over. In fact, it's just beginning. You were created on purpose. You were redeemed at a great price. And you are deeply, eternally loved.

Christ is not just part of your life now, He is your life. Let Him be your Lord, and you'll be fulfilled more than you thought possible. When He is your King, your kingdom is filled with righteousness, peace, and joy in the Holy Spirit. In Him you get to live, and move, and have your being. What a life of glory and promise.

Pursue Him. Seek Him. Follow Him.

You'll find that He is always better, always deeper, always closer than you could have ever imagined. And you'll spend the rest of your life and all of eternity discovering the unending depths of His love.

I'm so glad to be on this journey with you, and our stories to briefly connect on this side of eternity. Welcome to the journey.

"Therefore, if anyone is in Christ, he is a new creation; old things have passed away; behold, all things have become new." 2 Corinthians 5:17

Chapter 29

The Master Builder

By Mandy Adair

I first met Pastor Mandy Adair in ministry school, and God has used her voice tremendously in my journey back to Him. She carries an anointing to declare truth that breaks chains, and I'm honored to share her words with you here.

I have decided to follow Jesus! ...Now what? The moment we are born again, we become a child of God and a citizen of Heaven. By the power of the Holy Spirit, we are delivered out of the realm of darkness, and we are translated into a brand-new Kingdom of light, where Jesus reigns as eternal King.

If you've ever ventured into another country, you may quickly recognize the differences between the customs, language, and overall culture. On our first trip to Japan, my husband and I were shocked to realize there were no English signs at the airport where we landed. This was even more alarming because we were traveling without a group or translator, and we had a tight connection to make it to our destination. A thousand questions raced through my mind as we desperately searched for someone who looked as American as we did. We managed to find an airline employee who spoke enough English to direct us to our gate. Sweaty and stressed to the max, we made it just in time to board the aircraft. Crisis averted.

Once we come into the Kingdom of God, we are expected to learn it's laws, culture, and language. A failure to do so will result in delay, diversion, or most tragically missing our destination. The Bible, and most specifically, the New Testament, is the manual of God's Kingdom, introducing us to our new Father, our new family, our new identity, and our new purpose. Within its pages, we learn the laws, the currency, the customs, the values, and the language of our new homeland.

The Apostle Paul pleads with believers:

"Don't copy the behavior and systems of this world but let God transform you into a new person by changing the way you think. Then you will learn to know God's will for you, which is good and pleasing and perfect." (Romans 12:2 NLT)

The blood of Jesus is the cleansing agent for sin, and the only possible means to save the spirit of man. Once a person believes in their heart and confesses Jesus to be Lord (Romans 10:10) their spirit comes alive. We call this being "saved." But this isn't the final stage in the life of a believer- it's only the beginning.

It's the entry point to a vast, eternal Kingdom where we are called to go from one level of faith to the next, from one level of strength to the next, and from one level of glory to the next in an unending cycle that spans eternity. Paul is writing and urging the church of Rome to stop living like Romans and begin living like citizens of a new realm-but to do so will require them to change their thought processes, perspectives, and reasonings.

The apostle James puts it this way:

> "Therefore lay aside all filthiness and overflow of wicked-ness, and receive with meekness the implanted word, which is able to save your souls." James 1:21 NKJV

Just as the blood cleansed and saved the spirit, the Word has the power to cleanse and save the soul (mind, will, and emotions). Just as the spirit was made new, the mind must undergo a similar and just as drastic transformation. The Bible calls this process "the renewing of the mind," and this process is to last the rest of our days on the earth, is to become our greatest endeavor, our highest aim, and will determine our usefulness in the Kingdom of God.

To the Christian, this is the make or break, the do-or die. The importance you place on this process will determine everything about your future, your eternal reward, genera-tional legacy, and final destination. If that sounds high stakes and a bit heavy, good. We are repeatedly commanded in the epistles to think soberly about the high calling on our lives as members of God's family and citizens of His King-dom. The good news is this...God has provided supernat-ural assistance for us to tackle the project of mind renewal. He doesn't require us to figure it out on our own (like my husband and I in Japan), nor does He expect us to do it overnight.

> "By his divine power, God has given us everything we need for living a godly life." (2 Peter 1:3 NLT)

As it pertains to the renewing of the mind, our greatest asset is the Word of God. Have you ever lived through the saga of a home renovation? It usually begins with a need or desire- maybe more space, a new vision for current space, or possibly a critical need to deal with structural issues.

Several years ago, we returned to our Kentucky home after a week spent in Tampa, Florida to the unpleasant discovery of a flooded first story and basement. Once the initial cleanup was finished, we selected new flooring and began counting down the days until we'd be back in our home. We had 4 young children at the time, so this was more than a slight inconvenience. Little did I know how inconvenient it would become! The flooring crew discovered major structural problems with our home and recommended that it undergo a complete re-working of main support beams and everything that entails.

It entailed months of us living elsewhere...with four young children. It involved tearing out all the rotten, termite damaged beams, lots of measuring, calculating, planning, fitting, nailing, lifting, pounding, sweating, and possibly a few tears (they were mine). There were delays, standstills, setbacks. There was tension, friction, and it was costly. But there was a vision- a blueprint-a goal to attain. So, the construction crew kept at it until the structure they were standing on matched the plan before them.

When Paul penned the words of Romans 12:2, he used the Greek word "anakainosis" which means "a renewal-a renovation-a complete change for the better."

The renewing of the mind is best described as a comprehensive renovation of your emotions, thoughts, opinions, priorities, and will. It doesn't happen automatically, accidentally, or immediately, but the individual who keeps the blueprint in front of their eyes and the hammer of the

Word in their clutch will enjoy the soundness of mind and fullness of life that a strong structure allows. Jeremiah 23:29 says that the Word of God is like a hammer.

Every person who is born again comes into the Kingdom with faulty structures erected in their minds-structures formed by abuse, negligence, pride, ignorance, rejection, hatred, the list goes on. Those structures cannot hold the weight of God's eternal truths and purposes. Old, corrupt structures become limits that restrict the believer from walking in the newness of life that has been purchased by the redemption.

Someone who has been hurt or betrayed will often struggle to form relationships in the church for fear of another disappointment. This emotional structure will limit them from deep, life-giving fellowship that will foster spiritual growth and development. Someone else tends to be a know-it-all and is slow to listen to authority. In the Kingdom, that's a death wish. Another new believer comes from a lifestyle of moral relativism-where there is no standard of truth. Jesus makes the bold claim that He is the truth. These three individuals have different stories, families, and personalities, but they will all have to take the hammer of God's word to violently attack the old, faulty structures of thought based in human wisdom, personal experience, secular culture, and even religious tradition. Why?

What's the harm in a few faulty beams? I'm glad you asked. Paul answers:

> "For to be carnally minded is death...because the carnal mind is enmity against God." (Romans 8:6-7 NKJV)

This is strong language! Carnal, worldly thinking is an enemy of God and His purposes. Considering this, how much carnal thinking can we tolerate and be ok? Every time we read the Word or hear the Word taught or preached, we are not only being confronted with truth but also armed with a power-tool. We're gifted with a tool that is stronger than human reasoning, pride, insecurity, perversion, bitterness, and rejection.

God's Word is a hammer that, consistently applied to the hard rock, will shatter it in pieces. In 2 Corinthians 10:4, Paul writes, "The weapons we fight with...have divine power to demolish strongholds."

The popular tv series, "Fixer Upper" has a mass audience of viewers who live vicariously through Chip Gaines and his crew as they embark on "demo day'- the first day of the renovation where they demolish old walls, cabinets, and structures to prepare the home for a brand-new vision. It's a high-energy, physically taxing day of pulling out the old to make way for the new. So it is with renewing the mind- it takes concentrated effort and perseverance. It takes a commitment to the vision, a commitment that won't compromise for the sake of convenience or when weariness sets in.

The vision (God's blueprint) can only be fulfilled by taking God's Word and using it like a hammer to tear down every thought, perspective, and feeling that contradicts God's wisdom. Every faulty beam and every warped frame must be destroyed and cleared away to make room for something far more beautiful, useful, and pleasing to take shape. Your pastor can't do this for you, and God won't. You can't get in a prayer line, fire tunnel, or receive an impartation to get this job done. You've got to take the Word and apply it. Do it when you don't feel like it. Speak it when your feelings are raging and trying to lead you astray. Obey the Word without excuse. Every act of obedience is another swing of the hammer against that wrong feeling or thought. Eventually, it will break!

Once we have demolished the old framework in any given area of thought (relationships, identity, finances, etc), we begin the process of framing. The frame of a home are all the components that provide structural support-things like floor joists, beams, roof trusses. Correctly placed, these elements provide safety and ensure the longevity of the structure.

Hebrews 11: 3 says,

> "By faith, we understand that the worlds were framed by the word of God..." (NKJV);

The account of creation's story in Genesis reveals how everything we now see, touch, hear, and feel, came into being: God's spoken word. Again, John tells us in his gospel how all things came to be:

> "In the beginning the Word already existed. The Word was with God, and the Word was God. He existed in the beginning with God. God created everything through him, and nothing was created except through him." (John 1:1-3 NLT)

When God decided to create the cosmos, he did so with spoken words-and those words released His omnipotence; out of void and darkness came light, seas, land, sky, creatures, and vegetation. With nothing but His Word, He made all things visible and invisible with one exception-humanity- which he formed out of dust.

Because He is eternal, His Word is eternal. His eternal Word is sustaining the entire colossal universe-the writer of

Hebrews tells us that ALL things are upheld by the Word of His power! The written Word of God has been preserved and afforded to us for the purpose of creating a new framework of thought, but not merely human thought or worldly wisdom.

Words that contain omnipotence have been passed down through generations via the Bible; words that believed, spoken, and acted upon, release the same creative force and energy that was released in original creation; words that are capable of framing and holding your life together no matter what weight or pressure is applied. When you read and agree with God's word, you are laying floor joists, setting beams, and installing eternal structure that cannot be eroded by any earthly elements or demonic power.

Every time you act on or speak God's word, you are reinforcing your entire person-spirit, soul, and body. Reading, speaking, and doing the Word causes you to think like God! His Word is His will, His counsel, His way, His thoughts, His purposes revealed; the more you order your life according to scripture, the less you will reason like the world or agree with its systems.

When it's time to make a big decision, you won't consult selfish ambition, you will remember the words of Jesus: "Seek first the Kingdom of God." When someone hurts or betrays you, you'll recall his command, "Love your enemies." When you're tempted to worry about money, His words will echo in your spirit, "Do not worry about your life." You will find His words often contradict the ways of the world that we define as "common sense." But you will also find that when you come into agreement with His Words through obedience, that His power is released into that area of your life! Where there was once anxiety, God's

Word will erect a beam of trust. Where bitterness and unforgiveness was found, God's word has laid a floor joist of mercy. As you consistently read, speak, and obey the Bible, you will build a new framework of thoughts, emotions, desires, and identity.

Your entire personality will begin to reflect the blueprint of your Creator; and it will be more beautiful, more satisfying, and more rewarding than you can imagine.

In Matthew 7, Jesus tells the story of two men. The first man was a hearer of the Word. He may have been entertained by the minister; he may have even verbally agreed to the Word preached. But once the feeling of excitement wore off, he went on with life as usual. He never applied the Word in his own life. Jesus said this man built his house on the sand-and when a terrible storm rose and attacked this man's house, it fell because it had no fixed foundation.

The second man, like the first, heard the Word preached. But he went a step further and took the message to heart, putting it into practice. *He was a doer of the Word*. Jesus said that this man, the doer, built his house on a rock. When the storm hit his house, it stood firm.

Whether you're just beginning your journey with Jesus, or if you're somewhere in the middle, decide that you will not just be a reader or hearer of the Word. That's only the starting point.

With eyes of faith, see into the plan of God for your life —see that He desires to work with you to transform every part of your current existence into something that reflects His power, goodness, and glory.

He is a wise master builder. If you simply commit to his blueprint, He will build you into an *unshakeable house*.

My Dear Friend,

The testimony of Jesus is the spirit of prophecy and what He has done for me, He can do for you or for your parent, child, spouse, or even your dearest friend. No life is too far gone. No heart is too hardened. No story is beyond His pen.

As you turn this final page, I pray my journey leaves you with a living hope that anything is possible with God, and awakens a faith in you that refuses to let go until His promise is fulfilled. If someone you love has wandered, keep praying. Heaven hears you. God's heart beats for their return, and I am living proof that prayer works.

No matter what it looks like right now, it is not the end. It may appear lifeless, but so did I. He is the Resurrection. He still breathes into what the world calls dead. So whether you're standing for a lost child, a struggling marriage, a broken friendship, or a heart too heavy to lift, hold fast to His word. He will be faithful, always, and to the very end.

You're dearly loved,

Danica Reddy

Acknowledgements

I am overwhelmed with gratitude for the many people whose love, prayers, and encouragement carried me through the writing of this book. I could never name you all, but please know how deeply thankful I am.

Pastor Micah Wood and Delana—you saw me in my pain, sat with me in it, and prayed me through. Micah, your foreword and constant pointing me back to Jesus will stay with me forever. Pastors Jason and Mandy Adair—you spoke to who I was becoming, not where I had been, and your kindness gave me courage to keep going. Your continued friendship means the world to me. Dr. Marocco, Pastor Colleen, the Hughes family, and the Joneses—thank you for your leadership, covering, and steady anchor in this season. To the King's church family, you have been a refuge and a place of revival.

To my parents—thank you for raising me in the way I should go. Even when I wandered, the foundation you built remained. To my husband and children—you are my greatest earthly gifts. Kids, your joy reminds me daily to pursue Jesus with everything I have. Sri, thank you for standing by me through it all and giving me space to heal and grow.

To my Indian community—thank you for embracing me as one of your own. Even when some didn't fully understand, you're a gift to me.

Carly Mellini—your creativity brought this cover to life,

thank you for that and for being a good friend. Kalyn, Keirstyn, and Taylor—your steady faith through tears, prayers, and hard conversations has been a constant. Brittany, thank you for walking with me through the whirlwind.

To those who have run with me in ministry and missions—thank you for believing in the call of God on my life, even when I had forgotten it. To Valerie, my editor, and those who offered thoughtful feedback—your care helped shape these pages into what they are.

And to you, the reader—thank you for holding this book in your hands. My hope is that somewhere in these pages you've encountered Jesus—His mercy, His truth, and His relentless love. If He can rewrite my story, He can rewrite yours too.

About the Author

Danica Reddy is a wife, mother, and writer who has known both the heights of ministry and the depths of personal brokenness. After years of global missions and full-time ministry, she found herself far from the God she once served until mercy called her home. Her story is one of rescue, restoration, and the relentless love of Jesus.

Through her writing and teaching, Danica seeks to point others not to perfection, but to the God who resurrects what we think is too far gone. She now lives out her "yes" to Jesus daily—in motherhood, in ministry, and in the quiet, surrendered places most people never see. You can keep up more with her at www.livingoutyouryes.com.